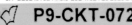

"From the first ten seconds of skimming, Sam's riveting stories sucked me right in. This is the most down-to-earth, inspiring, and action-able(!) book I've ever seen about how to get people's attention."
—**Derek Sivers, TED speaker on "First Follower" and founder of CD Baby**

"Not only is it possible to influence with integrity; it's preferable. This book shows how."
—**Dr. Joan Fallon, founder of Curemark and winner of a 2014 Gold Stevie Award for "Maverick of the Year"**

"Sam's new book is everything she recommends: true, new, efficient, engaging, Interactive, and _actionable_. Sam lives all of these things, and she's given us a guide to do so, too!"
—**Robert Wolcott, cofounder and Executive Director, Kellogg Innovation Network, Kellogg School of Management**

"Sam Horn is the best listener—and conversationalist—I know. This will help anyone establish connections at work and at home."
—**Mariah Burton Nelson, Vice President of Innovation and Planning, American Society of Association Executives**

"Looking for innovative ways to explain what you do and get across the value of what you have to offer? This book is for you."
—**Saul Kaplan, founder of Business Innovation Factory**

"Don't even think about preparing a pitch, proposal, or presentation without first reading _Got Your Attention?_"
—**Kay Koplovitz, founder of USA Networks and cofounder and Chairman, Springboard Enterprises**

"Powerful insights on how to build a movement that lasts and create authentic connections with volunteers, donors, strategic partners, and anyone who interacts with your brand."
—**Adam Braun, founder of Pencils of Promise**

"A must-read for anyone in the workplace who wants to contribute at the highest level and create more strategic networks."
—**Betsy Myers, former Executive Director, Center for Public Leadership, Harvard Kennedy School**

"Sam Horn asks and answers the question so many of us are struggling with: What does it take to really connect with people in a culture of impatience and alienation? A user-friendly gem."
—**Elizabeth Lesser, cofounder of Omega Institute and author of *Broken Open***

"These accessible techniques transcend generations and read like a modern-day version of *How to Win Friends and Influence People*."
—**Miki Agrawal, one of *Forbes*'s "Top 20 Millennials on a Mission" and founder of THINX**

"Thought-provoking insights on how to be clear and concise."
—**Roger Hunter, Project Manager and TEDxUGA speaker**

"I've interviewed Sam on my show. She rocks and so does this book."
—**John Lee Dumas, founder and host of the podcast, *Entrepreneur on Fire***

"Whether you're pitching, presenting, promoting, or persuading, you need to know how to be heard above the din. Sam Horn's smart and snappy book will teach you how to get people's attention—and keep it."
—**Daniel H. Pink, author of *To Sell Is Human* and *Drive***

"If you can't get people's attention, you'll never get their business. Sam Horn's new book shows how to quickly earn attention and respect so people are motivated to listen."
—**Terry Jones, founder of Travelocity, Founding Chairman of Kayak.com, and Chairman of WayBlazer**

"Every entrepreneur, executive, and educator will benefit from reading this brilliant book."
—**Amy Wilkinson, former White House Fellow and author of *The Creator's Code***

"Do you want to be a more compelling communicator? Sam shows you innovative ways to initiate genuine conversations and create meaningful connections that will help you turn strangers into friends."
—**Keith Ferrazzi, author of *Never Eat Alone* and the #1 *New York Times* bestseller *Who's Got Your Back***

"In today's increasingly disengaged workplace, these techniques for engaging employees and customers by focusing on their needs and priorities *first*...are a must for every leader."
—**Marshall Goldsmith, *Thinkers 50* Top Ten Global Business Thinker**

GOT YOUR ATTENTION?

How to Create Intrigue and Connect with Anyone

Sam Horn

BK

Berrett–Koehler Publishers, Inc.
a BK Business book

Berrett-Koehler Publishers, Inc.
1333 Broadway, Suite 1000
Oakland, CA 94612-1921
Tel: (510) 817-2277   Fax: (510) 817-2278   www.bkconnection.com

Ordering Information

Quantity sales. Special discounts are available on quantity purchases by corporations, associations, and others. For details, contact the "Special Sales Department" at the Berrett-Koehler address above.

Individual sales. Berrett-Koehler publications are available through most bookstores. They can also be ordered directly from Berrett-Koehler: Tel: (800) 929-2929; Fax: (802) 864-7626; www.bkconnection.com

Orders for college textbook/course adoption use. Please contact Berrett-Koehler: Tel: (800) 929-2929; Fax: (802) 864-7626.

Orders by U.S. trade bookstores and wholesalers. Please contact Ingram Publisher Services, Tel: (800) 509-4887; Fax: (800) 838-1149; E-mail: customer.service@ingrampublisherservices.com; or visit www.ingrampublisherservices.com/Ordering for details about electronic ordering.

Berrett-Koehler and the BK logo are registered trademarks of Berrett-Koehler Publishers, Inc.

Printed in the United States of America

Berrett-Koehler books are printed on long-lasting acid-free paper. When it is available, we choose paper that has been manufactured by environmentally responsible processes. These may include using trees grown in sustainable forests, incorporating recycled paper, minimizing chlorine in bleaching, or recycling the energy produced at the paper mill.

Library of Congress Cataloging-in-Publication Data
Horn, Sam.
Got your attention? : how to create intrigue and connect with anyone /
   by Sam Horn. -- First edition.
     pages cm
   Includes bibliographical references.
   ISBN 978-1-62656-250-9 (pbk.)
   1. Interpersonal communication. 2. Persuasion (Psychology) 3. Interpersonal
relations. 4. Success. I. Title.
   BF637.C45H674 2015
   650.1'3--dc23

                                                                    2014041888
First Edition
20 19 18 17 16 15   10 9 8 7 6 5 4 3 2 1

Interior design and project management: Dovetail Publishing Services
Cover design: Dan Tesser, Studio Carnelian
Author photo: Aliyah Dastour, Alimond Photography Studio

Dedication to Dale Carnegie

I never met you in person, but your classic book *How to Win Friends and Influence People* has influenced my entire life.

As a young teenager struggling to find my place in the world, I stumbled across your enduring insight,

> *"We can make more friends in two months by becoming interested in other people, than we can in two years by trying to get people interested in us."*

The essential rightness of those words settled in my soul and have shaped my interactions ever since.

Your book is testimony to the truth that books change lives.

It may be optimistic, even bordering on hubris, to hope this book has half the impact as yours, but a woman can dream. :-)

The premise of *Got Your Attention?* is a nod to your original advice,

> *"We can make more connections in two months by becoming intrigued in other people, than we can in two years by trying to get people intrigued in us."*

That is what I hope people take away from this, that they know it in their heart and apply it in their life.

Thank you.

Contents

What Is INTRIGUE and Why Is It Important?

I think the one lesson I have learned is that there
is no substitute for paying attention.

TV ANCHOR DIANE SAWYER

Did you know goldfish, yes, goldfish, have longer attention spans than we humans do?

Nine seconds to our eight. At least that's what Harvard Business School researcher Nancy F. Koehn reported in a February 2014 *Marketplace Business* article.[1]

It gets worse. *Fast Company* reported in March 15, 2012, that one in four people abandon a website if it takes longer than *four seconds* to load. And Drs. Jacqueline Olds and Richard Schwartz reported in the *Utne Reader,* "Two recent studies suggest our society is in the midst of a dramatic and progressive slide toward disconnection."[2]

Clearly, we have an impatience epidemic, and we're suffering from alienation and attention bankruptcy, all at the same time.

That's a problem because if you can't get people's attention, you'll never get their connection. The good news is, there are ways to overcome people's impatience, alienation, and chronic distraction, and this book teaches them.

If You Can't Get People's Attention, You'll Never Get Their Connection

I have found if you love life, life will love you back.

MUSICIAN ARTHUR RUBENSTEIN

I love this topic and want you to love it back, so, I'm going to follow Carrie Fisher's advice. Remember her? Princess Leia in *Star Wars*? Cinnamon-bun ears? Yes, that Carrie. She said, "Instant gratification takes too long."

Carrie's right. We don't want more information. We want to be intrigued ... and we want to be intrigued *fast*. That is why I'm going to share a quick backstory as to how and why I discovered and developed the INTRIGUE approach, then we'll jump into the how-to's. Sound good? Great. Here's the backstory.

I had the privilege of emceeing the Maui Writers Conference for seventeen years. We did something unprecedented at that time, which was to give authors an opportunity to jump the chain of command and connect face to face with publishing insiders. What we didn't anticipate was that these authors didn't know how to connect with these decision-makers. In fact, one woman exited her meeting with tears in her eyes. I asked, "Are you okay?"

She said, "No, I'm not okay. I just saw my dream go down the drain."

"Ouch. What happened?"

"I've been working on my book for three years. I put it on the table, the editor took one look at it, and said, 'I don't have time to read all that. Tell me in sixty seconds what your book is about and why someone would want to read it.'

"My mind went blank. I thought it was my job to write it. I thought it was his job to sell it. The more I tried to explain it, the more confused he became. My big chance, and I blew it."

I told her, "You still have an opportunity to connect with agents and editors. Many of them will be at our reception tonight, and you can meet them there."

The next day, I saw her in the halls and asked, "Did you have a chance to connect with some agents and editors last night?"

She wouldn't look at me. I thought maybe she hadn't heard me so I asked again.

With her head down, she said in a soft voice, "I didn't go."

Inside I'm thinking, *You worked on your book for years, spent thousands of dollars, flew across a continent and an ocean to get here, had a chance to meet decision-makers who had the power to make your dreams come true, and you didn't go?*

She said, "I was so intimidated. I didn't know what to say. I hid out in my hotel room."

Wow. She wasn't the only one who didn't get a deal that first year. Many other authors failed to get interest in their projects. The more I thought about it, the more I realized it wasn't that their projects didn't have value; it was because they didn't know how to connect with ecision-makers and quickly and compellingly communicate that value so they got it and wanted it.

I thought, *Somebody's got to do something about this.* I realized, *I'm as much a somebody as anybody*; I'll *do something about this.*

So, I wrote POP! *Create the Perfect Pitch, Title, and Tagline for Anything.* That book has been featured on MSNBC, in the *New York Times* and *Fast Company*, and has helped people create successful brand names, best-selling titles, and innovative marketing slogans.

I'm proud of the difference that book's made; however, I've realized in the past few years that it takes more than a clever title and tagline to connect with people. Titles and taglines can *catch* people's favorable attention; they can't *hold* it. If you really want to connect with people, you need to be able to *keep* their favorable attention and *gift* them with yours.

There Is NO Connection
without Quality Attention

Only connect.

NOVELIST E. M. FORSTER

I believe, at my core, that Forster's advice to "only connect" is true. When we look back, at the end of our life, what will matter is: Did we genuinely connect with the people important to us?

Yet so often, despite our best intentions and efforts, we *don't* connect. It's not that we don't want to; it's that we're not taught to. We're taught math, science, and history, yet we're not taught how to create mutually rewarding connections. As a result, we don't do it well or we don't do it at all.

The result? A profound sense of disconnection. Our ideas go unheard. Our projects go unfunded. Our programs go unattended. Our dreams go unfulfilled. Our relationships go...nowhere.

As Stephen Marche said in an April 2012 *Atlantic* article titled *Is Facebook Making Us Lonely?* "We suffer from unprecedented alienation. We have never been more detached from one another."

I asked myself, *What does it take to really connect with people in a culture of impatience and alienation?* Well, there has to be *two-way* attention for our interactions to be mutually rewarding. How do we do that? We stop trying to *get* attention and start *giving* attention.

It makes sense, doesn't it? If we want people to give us their precious time and attention, we must first give them ours. We go first. We set the precedent. Being intrigued *in* others makes us intriguing *to* others. Mutual INTRIGUE is the key to turning frustrating, waste-of-time, one-way communications into productive, rewarding two-way connections.

How to Make the Most of This Book

What did we go back to before there were drawing boards?

COMEDIAN GEORGE CARLIN

I've distilled everything I've learned about this topic into an easy-to-apply INTRIGUE acronym. Think of it as a recipe for connection. Each letter of INTRIGUE represents an ingredient that can help you create reciprocated favorable attention, which *is* the core of connection. As with any recipe, adapt it to your taste and situation.

I imagine you're busy, so I've kept the chapters under ten pages so you can dip in and derive value even when you have only a few minutes to spare. The Action Questions at the end of each chapter can help you and your team discuss how to customize these ideas to your priorities.

Speaking of priorities—the best way to benefit from this book is to fill out the W5 Form on the next page. Keeping your W5 Form, the INTRIGUE version of a "drawing board," in front of you while you work through the chapters switches you from *observer* mode ("That's a good idea") to *activator* mode ("Here's how I'll apply that idea") so you reap real-world results.

The W5 Form is a tangible way to focus your attention on who you want to connect with, beforehand. It helps you imagine: What will make this communication intriguing, useful, and relevant? What are the current problems, needs? How can I quickly address those and add value from the beginning so people are motivated to give me their valuable time and attention? Filling out your W5 Form is one of the single best things you can do to prepare for interactions that benefit all involved.

W5 Form:
Your Drawing Board for Preparing Intriguing Interactions

If we want to connect, we must first earn attention and respect.

Sam Horn

Taking the time to fill out this W5 Form can help you prepare mutually intriguing interactions.

WHAT is an upcoming situation for which you want to prepare?

Conference presentation? Staff meeting? Job interview? Book? Funding pitch? Proposal? Web copy? Ad campaign?

....

....

....

WHO is your intended audience?

What is their age, gender, background? What is their level of interest or resistance? What are their problems/unmet needs? What is their mood? (Impatient? Angry? Skeptical? Eager? Busy?) Describe them so you can clearly picture them.

....

....

....

WHERE and WHEN will this take place?

Your client's office at 9:00 AM? Dinner at a noisy restaurant? A Monday morning newsletter to your mailing list? A business luncheon in a hotel ballroom? An international Skype call and everyone's in different time zones?

....

....

....

WHY will this be an ROI for your decision-makers?

Why will they want to give you their attention? Why will they find this a productive use of their precious time, mind, and dime? How will this benefit them, produce bottom-line results for them?

....

....

....

WHY will this be an ROI for you?

What are three specific things you'd like to happen as a result of this interaction? What are three possible outcomes or actions that would make this a tangible success for you, your priority and business?

....

....

....

Part I

INTRIGUE

I = INTRO

Open with an INTRO that Has People at Hello

I'm afraid of nothing except being bored.

ACTRESS GRETA GARBO

Garbo's not the only one afraid of being bored.

People today are impatient.

Their internal clock starts ticking the moment you start talking.

They're wondering, "Will you be a bore, snore, or chore?"

If they don't see or hear something in the first minute (or first page) that earns their favorable attention; It's NEXT and they're on to something else.

In this section, you'll discover a variety of ways to craft openings that have people at hello.

Keep your W5 Form in front of you as you read these chapters so you can be thinking about which of these openings would earn people's interest and motivate them to put things aside and make you their top priority.

Chapter 1

Ask "Did You Know?" Questions

*It's not overly dramatic to say your destiny
hangs on the impression you make.*
TV JOURNALIST BARBARA WALTERS

It's daunting, isn't it, to think the destiny of something you care about depends on your ability to create a favorable impression for it in the first minute?

That was how Kathleen Callendar, founder of PharmaJet, felt when she told me, "I've got good news and I've got bad news. Springboard Enterprises is giving me an opportunity to pitch to a room full of investors at the Paley Center in New York City."

I told her, "That is good news. Springboard has helped female entrepreneurs like Robin Chase of ZipCar receive more than $6.4 billion dollars in funding. What's the bad news?"

"I'm going at 2:30 and I have only ten minutes. You can't say anything in ten minutes. How can I possibly explain our team credentials, clinical trials, and financial projections in ten minutes?"

"Kathleen, you don't have ten minutes. Those investors will have heard sixteen other pitches. You have sixty seconds to break through the afternoon blahs and earn their attention."

Here is the intro we crafted that not only helped Kathleen win buy-in and funding, it helped her be named one of *BusinessWeek's* most promising social entrepreneurs of 2010.[3]

Did you know there are 1.8 billion vaccinations given every year?

*Did you know up to half of those vaccinations are given with
reused needles?*

Did you know we are spreading and perpetuating the very diseases we're trying to prevent?

Imagine if there was a painless, one-use needle for a fraction of the current cost.

You don't have to imagine it, we've created it. It's called PharmaJet, as this article shows . . .

And she was off and running. Are you intrigued? So was everyone in that room.

Let's put this in perspective. The PharmaJet team used to open their presentations by explaining they were a "platform for a medical delivery device for subcutaneous inoculations."

Yikes. That intro would have *lost* people at hello. Yet that is how many people open their communications, with blah-blah-blah explanations that cause listeners to think "duh" or "huh?" They've already concluded this is "hard work," and they switch their attention to something more enjoyable or urgent. Kathleen had a competitive advantage because, one minute in, everyone was already curious and eager to know more.

How Else Can the "Did You Know?" Intro Be Used?

You can't just give someone a creativity injection. You have to create an environment for curiosity.

#1 RATED TED TALKER SIR KEN ROBINSON

In case you're wondering if you can use this opening online and in print, as well as in person, the answer is a resounding yes. If fact, you may choose to follow Sean Keener's example. Sean and his BootsnAll team used a "Did you know?" opening in a sixty-second video posted on the home page of their website. He tells me it has helped their new product, Indie, become an instant success. His intro starts with:

> *Did you know you used to need a travel agent to book a multi-city trip with five stops?*
>
> *Did you know it used to take up to forty-eight hours to book a five-stop trip?*
>
> *Did you know it used to take up to five days to receive a price quote for a five-stop trip?*
>
> *Imagine, if for the first time ever, you could plan and book a five-stop trip yourself, without ever having to use a travel agent?*
>
> *Imagine if you could get your own price quotes for a multi-stop trip?*
>
> *Imagine if you could do all the above in less than an hour?*
>
> *You don't have to imagine it; we've created it. It's called* Indie.[4]

Intrigued? So have been the thousands of people who have watched that video and were sufficiently intrigued to click on the link to find out more.

Ready for an example of how this opening can be used in print? Imagine you're writing an e-book on how to get hired in today's tough job market. You could start with this opening:

Did you know that:

♦ *Of the 3.6 million job openings in 2012, 80 percent were never advertised?*

♦ *118 people (on average) apply for any given job and only 20 percent get interviews?*

♦ *In 2013 in the United States, 53.6 percent of bachelor's degree holders under the age of twenty-five were jobless or underemployed?*[5]

Imagine if you could:

- ◆ *Find out about quality jobs that were never advertised?*
- ◆ *Dramatically increase your likelihood of getting an interview this week?*
- ◆ *Learn ten new, yet proven ways to stand out in today's supercompetitive job market?*

You don't have to imagine it. This sixty-page e-book shares real-life success stories of individuals who found jobs in three months as a result of these techniques. In fact, . . .

Isn't that more interesting than most "tell 'em what you're going to tell 'em" openings that leave you thinking, **You're insulting my intelligence. Just get to it!** And in case you're curious, the statistics in this sample e-book copy are true. An Intrigue Agency team member found them, in less than five minutes, by GTS (Googling that Subject).

Three Steps to Crafting a "Did You Know?" Intro

Somewhere, something incredible is waiting to be known.
ASTRONOMER CARL SAGAN

Please get out your W5 Form so you can craft an opening that introduces something *your* decision-makers don't know so you can have them at hello.

Step 1: Open with three startlingly relevant "Did You Know?" questions

Introduce three things your decision-makers don't know, but would like to know, about the:

- ◆ Scope of the problem you've solving
- ◆ Urgency of the issue you're addressing

- Dramatic shift in a trend you're discussing
- Unmet need you're filling

Be sure to cite reputable sources, (e.g., *Wall Street Journal, Forbes*) to add gravitas and so people know you're not making up your numbers. No vague, sweeping generalizations; (i.e., "Millions of people are out of work" or "Unemployment is rampant"). Find out exactly how many people are out of work as of that month, so people trust your data and can trust you're telling the truth.

Are you thinking, *Where do I find these facts, experts, and verifiable statistics?* GTS–Google that Stuff. Use your favorite search engine to ask:

- What are shocking statistics about _____ (your subject)?
- What recent research has been done about _____ (your topic)?
- Who is an expert on _____ (your issue)?
- What are the most popular articles about _____ (your problem)?
- What are changing trends about _____ (your target market)?
- What are the best websites or most popular blogs _____ (your cause or industry)?

In minutes, you may discover a well-known think tank just released data that proves the problem you're addressing is growing exponentially and has more drastic consequences than anticipated.

You might find a study showing your target demographic is spending a growing percentage of their income on *your* type of product every year, and there are huge profits to be made.

The goal is to come up with startling "Really? That's news to me!" facts that affect the money, time, safety, convenience, health, performance, risk, or norms of the issue you're focusing on.

Craft those facts into three one-sentence "Did you know?" questions. Why only three? Some people think the more evidence they present, the more likely they are to get a yes. Wrong.

A May 7, 2011, *Newsweek* cover story entitled *Brain Freeze* reported that piling on information backfires because people shut down in the face of too much information.[6] They're not about to say yes to something they can't grasp. It's far more effective to cherry-pick the three most impressive aspects and make them as pithy as possible so people grasp them the first time they hear them.

Step 2: Use the word *imagine* linked with three "Who wouldn't want that?" attributes of your proposed solution.

The word *imagine* pulls people out of their preoccupation and helps them actively process what you're saying instead of passively hearing it. They're no longer distant. They're fully focused on you instead of distractedly thinking about the UPOs (unidentified piled objects) stacking up on their desk.

How do you come up with the three "Who wouldn't want that?" attributes? Think back to Kathleen Callendar and PharmaJet. What did her decision-makers care about? Those reused needles, so we emphasized they were "one use." No one likes painful inoculations, so we clarified they were "painless." Decision-makers always care about money, so we indicated her offering was "a fraction of the current cost." Do you see how we distilled her solution into a succinct ideal scenario that evoked a "Who wouldn't want that?" response? That's your goal.

Step 3. Transition with "You don't have to imagine it; we've created it. In fact. . . ."

Provide precedents and evidence so they know this isn't speculative or pie-in-the-sky; this is a done deal, and you and your team are ready to deliver it. Share a testimonial from a named client who vouches for you. Hold up an article that reports your results. Reference a benchmark showing what you're suggesting is not an unproven risk. It's been done before, successfully.

One final reason the "Did you know?" intro is so effective: All the above can be condensed into a rare and welcome sixty seconds. Other communicators are still telling the audience what they're going to tell them, and you have already earned their attention and respect and they're eager to hear more.

I hope you'll try this opening for your next high-stakes communication. It has made a dramatic difference for many of my clients, and I know it can help you connect with your decision-makers in record time.

Action Questions: Ask "Did You Know?" Questions

Are you doing what you're doing today because it works or because it's what you were doing yesterday?
TV HOST DR. PHIL MCGRAW

1. What's the situation on your W5 Form? Instead of telling people what you're going to tell them, how can you open by asking three "Did you know?" questions?

2. How will you help people picture your ideal scenario with the word *imagine* and distill three aspects of your proposed solution into a "Who wouldn't want that?" scenario?

3. How will you bridge into "You don't have to imagine it…" and provide empirical evidence so decision-makers know this isn't too good to be true; it is a done deal and you're ready to deliver it?

Chapter 2

Show Them the Fish

A lot of times people don't know what they
want until you show it to them.

ENTREPRENEUR STEVE JOBS

Jobs was right. People don't know unless you show them.

Here's what I mean. Did you read the book or see the movie *Jaws*? Do you know the backstory behind its iconic cover? Bantam Books president Oscar Dystel rejected the original cover, which simply depicted the word *Jaws* in white text on a black background. Dystel was afraid readers would think it was about a dentist. He ordered his design team back to the drawing board with the admonition, "I want to see that fish."

The designer came back with the famous image of a woman swimming in the ocean, unaware that a huge shark is lurking beneath her. That eye-catching image proved to be so popular that the film studio asked to use it for the movie poster. It may have been years since you've seen that cover art, but I bet you can still picture it in your mind.

That's the power of turning your idea into an image that tells its story. Not only is it more likely to capture people's attention, but it gives your idea staying power. Would *Jaws* have grossed more than $470 million and be one of the "top ten most successful movies of all time" without the memorable cover art that told the story in a single glance? I don't think so.

Act Out the Problem so They Want Your Solution

When you advertise fire extinguishers, open with the fire.
ADVERTISING LEGEND DAVID OGILVY

Entrepreneur Cari Carter understood the importance of "showing people the fish." Cari was participating in a competition called "The Dolphin Tank" (a kinder, more compassionate, version of the TV show *Shark Tank* or *The Dragon's Den* where entrepreneurs pitch their products to a panel of investors to win funding.)

As a judge, I had an opportunity to review Cari's business plan in advance. She had created a hook, called Cargo, you put in your car to hang your purse on. I thought, *Really?! You're building a business around a hook that holds a purse?*

Cari, however, intrigued everyone in the first minute. She carted a full-size car seat to the front of the room, set it down on the floor next to her, and put a purse on it. She stood up, faced the group, wrapped her fingers around an imaginary steering wheel, and started "driving" while saying:

> Have you ever been driving along and you had to STOP all of a sudden?

> Your purse falls off the passenger seat, and your cell phone falls out. You're scrabbling around trying to retrieve it and stay on the road, all at the same time? Imagine never having to worry about that again. Imagine having a hook that you . . .

At this point, a man stood up and said, "I'll take *two*. One for my wife and one for my daughter."

Wow. Cari went from a skeptical "Really?!" to an enthusiastic "I'll take *two*" in sixty seconds. That's the power of showing and asking. Cari did several smart things that contributed to her capturing and keeping everyone's attention.

1. She used a prop to help us see what she was saying.

I'm sure it was a hassle to haul that car seat into the Long Beach Convention Center. It was, however, well worth it because it created curiosity. We were all wondering, *What are you going to do with that?* Instead of being another "talking head," Cari had our attention *before* she even said hello.

2. She "made us look."

Our attention is where our eyes are. If we're not looking at a speaker, we're not listening to that speaker. Cari gave us something interesting to look at, so we focused on her instead of our digital devices.

3. She opened with the "fire."

Instead of describing her startup, she demonstrated a "fire" (a situation where things went wrong), which made us want her "fire extinguisher" (her solution to that situation). We remembered a time that happened to us or a loved one and voluntarily decided we wanted her product, so we could prevent that from happening again.

Don't Show and Tell, Show and Ask

*I believe that if you show people the problems and you
show them the solutions, they will be moved to act.*

PHILANTHROPIST BILL GATES

Many of us grew up doing "Show and Tell" in elementary school. A premise of INTRIGUE is "It's smarter to ask than tell. And it's even smarter to 'Show and Ask.'" Why? It verbally *and* visually engages your audience.

Here's another example of how "showing and asking" can help you win buy-in.

I was working with a client who had created a "receipt aggregator." A what?! Exactly. Anytime you tell someone about your product and you create confusion, you're better off turning your description into a demonstration. So that's how my client opened her presentation. She took a carry-on suitcase with her to the front of the room and rummaged around it while asking:

> *Have you ever returned home from a business trip, tried to track down your receipts, and couldn't find them anywhere?*
>
> *Or did you find crumpled-up pieces of paper like this (pulling up wadded-up, water-stained receipts) but couldn't make sense of them?*
>
> *Did you check all the pockets of your suitcase only to realize you're missing receipts for your biggest expenses?*
>
> *Did you know 67 percent of road warriors claim they haven't asked for reimbursement of travel expenses because they couldn't find the receipts?*
>
> *Wouldn't it be wonderful to never have to worry about that again? Imagine a . . .*

See how this works? Halfway through her opening, people were laughing because they identified with what she was saying. Asking "Have you ever?" or "Did you?" or "Wouldn't it be wonderful?" questions while acting out a frustrating situation is an effective way to win buy-in because people think, *Been there, done that, don't want to do it again.* You know you've connected when people say, "That just happened to me yesterday!" or "You're talking to *me*!"

"Show and Ask" Gets Eyebrows Up

The best thing you can do is surprise yourself.
COMEDIAN STEVE MARTIN

There's another reason "Show and Ask" is so effective. It gets people's eyebrows up.

What's this about getting eyebrows up? It's a tangible way to test if what you're saying is breaking through people's preoccupation and capturing their favorable attention.

Try it right now. Imagine someone is explaining what they do and they're not making sense. Knit and furrow your eyebrows. Do you feel frustrated, confused? That means you don't get what's being said. And if you don't get what's being said, the person talking won't get what they want because *confused people don't say yes.*

Now, keep your eyebrows neutral. If your eyebrows don't move, it means *you're* unmoved. What's being said isn't having any impact, it's not getting through.

Now, *lift* your eyebrows. Do you feel engaged, intrigued? Like you want to know more? That means what's being said just got in your mental door.

From now on, your goal is to get people's eyebrows up in the first minute of your interactions. It's a sure sign you've created curiosity (i.e., they want to know more) *and* it's an indication you've won their favorable attention.

Show Them the Face

You had my curiosity, but now you have my attention.
LEONARDO DICAPRIO'S CHARACTER IN QUENTIN
TARANTINO'S MOVIE *DJANGO UNCHAINED*

I was hired to help an IT exec prepare for his department's annual all-hands meeting. After he showed me his slide deck, I asked, "How do you want your employees to feel?"

Blink. Blink. *"Feel?"*

"Yes, feel."

"Umm, I guess I want them to feel proud. We exceeded all our numbers this year."

"What else?"

"Well, excited. We've got a new product launch in Q1 and some very ambitious goals."

"Do you think you might want to put some pictures of people in your deck?"

His PowerPoint slides consisted entirely of words, metrics, and graphs. Not one photo of the employees responsible for exceeding those quotas, for meeting those goals.

He was quick on the uptake and asked a company photographer to go around their offices and take pictures of team members who had contributed to their stellar year. He got back in touch the following week to say, "You should have seen what happened. People were cheering as they saw their co-workers on the screen, and everyone was high-fiving one another as they left the room."

That is the power of *showing the face*. And not generic clipart images pulled off the Internet. Why not (with their permission):

- Honor your employees by showing *their* photos at your annual meeting?
- Showcase your clients by featuring their faces on your website?
- Wrap up your convention on a high note by showing a montage of happy registrants so they can celebrate one another and the activities they just attended?
- Make your newsletter more intriguing by featuring candid shots of your members?

Film director Irvin Kershner (*Star Wars* trilogy) said, "There's nothing more interesting than the landscape of the human face." That's especially true when people know the face of the person being featured. If you want people's favorable attention, don't just share facts, share faces.

Want more ways to intrigue people and get their eyebrows up? Our next chapter introduces ways to give yourself a competitive advantage when you're competing for someone's attention.

Action Questions: Show Them the Fish

Tell me and I forget. Show me and I may remember. Involve me and I understand.

CONFUCIUS

1. Look at your W5 Form. How are you going to show people the fish? How are you going to turn your idea into an image so people see what you're saying?

2. How could you use props to act out a problem so people want your solution? How could you demonstrate your product so people witness the value of what you're offering?

3. How could you show and ask? What "Have you ever...?" or "Did you...?" questions could you act out to put people in a situation where they wish they had your product?

4. How can you honor employees, members, and customers by featuring their faces, with their permission, in your communications so they're more real and so they cause people to feel?

Chapter 3

Share What's Rare

Anyone who waits for recognition is criminally naive.
CONGRESSWOMAN BARBARA JORDAN

Many people are humble *to a fault* when trying to get their decision-makers' attention. Humility is a lovely trait but, taken to an extreme, it can become your Achilles' heel. Understand that business communication is a competition for your customers' attention. You can't afford to be subtle and wait for them to recognize your value. That's naive, idealistic, way too passive.

It's up to you to share what's rare so you're the one decision-makers notice. Your ability to do this can be a career-maker or career-breaker.

My son Tom is an excellent example of how taking responsibility for sharing how you're rare can help you land your dream job. Tom and his brother grew up in Maui, Hawaii. One starry night, we went out for our customary walk-and-roll. What's a walk-and-roll? I would walk the quiet streets of our neighborhood while the boys rode alongside on their skateboards or bikes. I asked Tom, "What do you want to be when you grow up?"

Tom pointed to the sky and said, "Something to do with up there."

Little could we have predicted Tom would one day graduate from Virginia Tech with degrees in aerospace engineering, physics, astronomy, and math. Suffice it to say, I didn't help him with his homework. Several weeks before graduation, Tom checked out the VT job board. He couldn't believe his eyes. There was an opening at NASA's Mission Control at Johnson Space Center. Remember the movie *Apollo 13* with Tom Hanks' character saying, "Houston, we've got a problem?" Yes, *that* Mission Control.

Tom eagerly filled out the application and asked me to take a look at it. It was impressive, but he had left out an achievement I thought could help his application stand out. I asked, "Tom, why didn't you mention you and your college team won that international competition to plan a manned mission to Mars?"

Guess what Tom said? *"But, Mom, that would be bragging."*

Arggh. I told him, "Tom, it's not bragging if you've done it. Put yourself in your decision-makers' shoes. They're going to receive hundreds of applications that *all look alike*. Everyone's got an impressive GPA, multiple majors, and extra-curricular activities. You need to figure out how you're *unlike* everyone else. If you've achieved something few others can claim, it may be the one thing that pops you out of the pack and motivates them to call you for an interview."

Tom included that credential, got the interview, and got the job. Now, every morning, he gets to go to work as a flight controller, working with the astronauts and the International Space Station. At least part of the reason Tom landed his dream job was because he shared a rare credential that helped him break out instead of blend into that stack of résumés.

What's Your Competitive Edge?

If you don't have a competitive advantage, don't compete.
FORMER GM CEO JACK WELCH

Do you have a situation coming up where you'll be applying for a job, position, or contract? What is something rare you could share? What could help you pop out of your pack?

◆ Where have you served in a leadership capacity and managed people to achieve an impressive, measurable goal in a specific amount of time?

- Where have you initiated a first-of-its-kind idea or project that added value to an organization, industry, or community?

- What awards or recognition have you received for your character, community service, volunteer efforts, or contributions to others?

- What is something uncommon you do in your personal life that could be a conversation-starter? Do you docent at a museum, windsurf, or volunteer at the humane society?

If you're asking someone to spend money on you (and that's what competing for a job, account, or contract represents), be sure to indicate how you're going to make money for them.

You've heard the phrase, "If you can't measure it, you can't manage it." Well, if you don't provide evidence of the measurable results you've produced for others, how can decision-makers trust you'll deliver measurable results for them?

Backing up your claims with specific examples of where you've saved, managed, or made money for previous employers, sponsors, and investors gives you a competitive edge because many job applicants give a laundry list of work experience; they never back up their claims with metrics.

If It's Obvious, It Isn't Intriguing

I told my doctor, "I broke my leg in two places."
He said, "Stop going to those places."
COMEDIAN HENNY YOUNGMAN

A bookkeeper in central California told me, "I understand it's important to share what's rare; I just don't know what's rare about me. I'm competing with more established businesses to win the account of the largest landowner in our area, and my credentials don't measure up to theirs."

If your competitors are national firms with big-name clients and you can't compete with that, *don't go there*. Going head-to-head with a competitor's strength is a losing battle.

Instead, emphasize you're a small shop with no layers of bureaucracy, so they can count on you to be *nimble*. If competitors are headquartered on the East Coast, emphasize you're an 8A (a woman-owned-and-operated business) and active in the local community. You may not be able to compete with their offices in twenty states, but they can't compete with the fact you were president of the local Chamber of Commerce and know all the business owners in town.

What's Your Commonality Edge?

When you're surrounded by people who share a passionate commitment around a common purpose, anything is possible.
STARBUCKS FOUNDER HOWARD SCHULTZ

Sometimes, the best way to get eyebrows up is not to focus on how you're different from your competitors; it's to focus on what you have in common with your decision-makers.

That's exactly what Leslie Charles did when preparing for a writers' conference. Leslie told me she wanted to be represented by Patti Breitman, who agented John Gray (*Men Are from Mars, Women Are from Venus*) and Richard Carlson (*Don't Sweat the Small Stuff*).

I asked her, "Why would Patti be intrigued by your book?"

"Well, people are under so much pressure these days; they tend to take their stress out on one another. My book introduces practical, proactive ways to deal with anger."

"That's good, Leslie. Now the question is, why would Patti choose to represent you because she has a full list and isn't really looking for new clients?"

Leslie looked at me, "I'm not sure how to answer that."

"Many authors think the key to landing a deal is to write a quality book. That's important, but there are a lot of quality books out there that don't get bought. Agents work "on spec." They don't make money unless your book makes money. You need to show how you will drive sales via an ambitious marketing plan, and it'd be smart to introduce an interest you and Patti share."

"You mean it doesn't matter that I've written a quality manuscript that will help a lot of people?"

"Of course, it matters; it just may not have been enough." I knew Leslie rode dressage (a specialized form of riding horses) so I suggested, "Add to your bio that you ride dressage."

Leslie gave me a puzzled look, "But that doesn't have anything to do with my book."

I smiled, "I know, but Patti rides dressage."

Patti and Leslie had a delightful meeting, connected over their common interest in dressage, and ended up working together. The moral of that story? Leslie was a first-time author. Patti was the world's most in-demand nonfiction agent at that time. What got Patti's attention wasn't just the potential of Leslie's project, it was the fact they shared a passion.

Quality, talent, and potential value are important. But your project may never see the light of day unless you introduce something in the first minute or page that gives you a:

1. *Competitive edge* because it is *unlike* everything else your decision-makers have seen

2. *Commonality edge* because it is *like* something your decision-makers care about

Either can help you win buy-in and win the race for your decision-makers' attention.

Action Questions: Share What's Rare

It's not enough to be perceived to be the best at what you do;
you must be considered the only one who does what you do.

Jerry Garcia of the rock band Grateful Dead

1. Time to review your W5 Form. What is something rare you can share to give yourself a competitive edge? What impressive credential will catch your decision-makers' attention? How are you the best at what you do or the only one who does what you do?

2. What achievement or experience can few of your competitors claim? How will you substantiate that claim with names and numbers so decision-makers can trust it's true?

3. What do you have in common with your decision-makers that could create a connection?

Chapter 4

Turn a No into a Yes

If you stick to what you know; you'll sell yourself short.
SINGER CARRIE UNDERWOOD

If you stick to what you know … you'll get a No. Instead, ask yourself, "Why will my decision-makers say No?" and say it *first*. Here's an example of someone who did this brilliantly.

Several years ago I went to the Business Innovation Factory (BIF) conference in Providence, Rhode Island. It was a fascinating couple of days with leading-edge innovators from around the world including Tony Hsieh of Zappos and Alan Webber of Fast Company.

The most impressive speaker was a surprise. She walked to the center of the stage and waited until she had everyone's attention. Then, with a big smile, she leaned out to the group and said, "I know what you're thinking. What's a thirteen-year-old going to teach me about innovation?"

She paused for a moment with a twinkle in her eye and said, "We thirteen-year-olds know a thing or two … like how to flip our hair." In thirty seconds, Cassandra Lin had everyone on her side.

Why? She read her audience's mind and realized these global thought-leaders might be a wee bit skeptical about her having anything of value to offer. So she brought it up first, and in doing so, won everyone over.

By the way, Cassandra continued to earn our attention and respect by describing how she and her fellow seventh-graders had taken a field trip to the sewers of Providence. They discovered they're filled to bursting with FOG—fat, oil, and grease. So she and her classmates founded

TGIF—"turn grease into fuel." Every Saturday, they collect FOG from restaurants and industrial parks, recycle it, and donate the money they receive to needy families. Go Cassandra.

How Can You Turn Resistance into Receptivity?

Never allow a person to tell you No who
doesn't have the power to say Yes.
FORMER FIRST LADY ELEANOR ROOSEVELT

What is that situation you identified on your W5 Form? Why will your decision-makers say, "You've got to be kidding?" Perhaps you're proposing an expensive program and you anticipate your boss will be thinking, *We don't have any money in our budget for this.*

Bring up your boss's objection by saying, "You may be thinking we don't have any money in our budget for this. If I can have your attention for the next three minutes, I'll point out where we can find that money and how we'll make it back in the first three months of this project."

Imagine you're suggesting a new membership recruitment program to your association board and predict they'll have their mental arms crossed because a similar program failed last year.

Open with, "You may be thinking we tried this before and it didn't work. You're right, and I've identified three mistakes we made last time and how to prevent them from happening this time."

Realize, if you don't voice naysayers' objections, they won't be listening; they'll be waiting for you to stop talking so they can tell you why this won't work.

What if My Decision-Makers Have Already Told Me No?

People can't believe you if they don't know what you're saying, and they can't know what you're saying if they're not listening, and they won't listen if you're not interesting.

ADMAN BILL BERNBACH

People also won't listen if they've told you No before. If they're thinking *No* in their mind, they'll never say Yes with their mouth ... unless you introduce new evidence that gives them a face-saving reason to revisit and reverse their previous decision.

That was the case with a workshop participant in Berlin who raised his hand and said, "What if we're trying to connect with someone who's turned us down in the past?"

I told him, "You can persuade people to give you a second chance if you acknowledge they've turned you down before and let them know circumstances have changed and you have new reasons they might want to reconsider. What's the situation?"

"We've just hired a professional player to coach my son's traveling soccer team, and we need to raise money for his salary. We're going to approach our local bookstore, but the owner gets asked for donations all the time. The standard offer to put the bookstore's name on our uniforms won't motivate him to agree to this because that doesn't drive business for him."

"Good for you for recognizing that's insufficient incentive. Open with, '*I can only imagine* you get asked for donations all the time.' That lets him know you're empathizing with what it must be like to get pressured to give to every worthy cause that walks in his door."

"What do I say next?"

"Jump into how you're going to make this a win for *him*. Say, 'Which is why I'd like to propose an event that draws people to your store, boosts your sales, and gives you lots of positive press.'"

Ari smiled and said, "That probably *would* get his interest."

"You're right. Then let him know you'd like to arrange for your soccer player-coach to sign his bestselling book on a day of his choice. Sweeten the pot by saying you've arranged for a team parent who's a professional photographer to take photos of the soccer pro with his customers in front of their logo for $10 a pop. That will make this a successful fundraiser for you and give him ongoing goodwill because those photos will stay on people's refrigerators for a long time. Continue to put yourself in the bookseller's shoes. What else would make this a win for him?"

Ari thought for a moment and then said, "I know. One of our team parents is a social media guru. She could blog, Tweet, and post this on Facebook so even more people show up."

"Good idea. That will put even more 'cheeks in the seats,' which will make this a revenue-producer for both of you. Notice, all these actions benefit the bookseller *and* your son's team. That's the beauty of this approach. Everyone wins."

Action Questions: Turn a No into a Yes

A man convinced against his will is of the same opinion still.
AUTHOR LAURENCE J. PETER

1. Look at your W5 Form. If you want decision-makers to give you a chance, figure out why they *won't* give you a chance and bring it up first.

2. Read your decision-makers' mind. Why will they be resistant? What have they already made up their mind about? How can you voice these objections so they're a nonissue?

3. Have these decision-makers told you No in the past? How can you acknowledge that up front with the words "I can only imagine," and then offer new evidence of why your request will benefit them so they have the incentive to reverse themselves and give you a chance?

Chapter 5

Psych Yourself Up, Not Out

I get nervous if I don't get nervous. I think it's healthy.
You just have to channel that into the show.

SINGER BEYONCÉ

An entrepreneur asked me, almost in a state of panic, "My laptop froze in the middle of a crucial presentation last week. It took me forever to get my slides working again, but by then it was too late. I'd lost everyone's attention and couldn't get them back. I've got another presentation coming up and I'm afraid of another meltdown. Can you help me regain my confidence?"

I asked her, "Are you an athlete?"

"Yes, but what does that have to do with regaining my confidence?"

"Because you've played sports, you know there are two kinds of athletes when the game's on the line. The kind who step back and say, 'DON'T give me the ball.' And the kind who step up and say, 'Give me the ball.'" I looked her straight in the eye and said, "I bet you're the latter."

She laughed and said, "You're right."

"That's why, from now on, you're going to see speaking as a sport so you can walk in and project a 'Gimme the ball' kind of confidence that helps you feel, look, and act like a winner."

Tennis champ Chris Evert was asked, on the first day of the tournament, if Serena Williams had a chance of winning the 2014 US Open. Chris said, "We all know confidence is the name of the game for her." Confidence is the name of the game for *all* of us. Fortunately, it is a learnable skill, not a mysterious ability we either have or don't. These four steps can help you channel nervousness into the "show," so you can walk into any interaction, raring to go.

See Communication as a Sport

She walks out like she expects to win. She looks like she belongs.

PATRICK McENROE, TALKING ABOUT FIFTEEN-YEAR-OLD
TENNIS PLAYER CICI BELLIS AT THE 2014 US OPEN

Here are the steps I shared with my client to help her psych herself up instead of out. Remember: you act in accordance with your expectations. Prepare for high-stakes communications just like you would a championship match. These steps can help you walk in expecting to command attention and respect and feeling and looking like you belong. This is not trivial. After all, how can people have confidence in you if you don't have confidence in yourself?

1. Go for a walk/rehearse.

Have you been told to practice what you want to say in front of a mirror? That's terrible advice! That focuses you on *you*, which makes you overly self-aware. It's smarter to get out of your head and get moving so you practice multifocus concentration.

What's multifocus concentration? It is that stream-of-conscious (versus self-conscious) flow in which athletes are able to stay focused while adapting to changing circumstances.

Think about it. Baseball players have to anticipate what pitch is coming, plan how to hit it while glancing to see if their teammate is stealing second base. Soccer players pass the ball to a running teammate while avoiding a defender and checking where the goalie is positioned.

How do you, as a communicator, get good at this multifocus concentration that pro athletes have mastered? You get out from behind that desk and get moving. A 2014 Stanford study found that "walking improves creative output by an average of 60 percent."[7]

When you walk/rehearse, you pay attention to the skateboarder and cyclist coming your way while crafting what you want to say. You're, literally and figuratively, getting good at thinking on your feet. You are envisioning how to get and keep your decision-makers' eyebrows up while adapting to your surroundings. That is the multifocus concentration state you want to be in when delivering that presentation, interviewing for that job, or negotiating that contract.

2. Have a flexible game plan.

Never, ever memorize a script or rely on reading from a teleprompter. That disconnects you from the group because it locks your attention on your notes or the screen. Why should your audience pay attention to *you* if you're not paying attention to *them*? Plus, if one thing goes wrong, you're lost because you're in your head instead of in the moment.

Communication is not about delivering prepared remarks verbatim. Intriguing communication is about connecting with people so you see the light go on in their eyes. It involves monitoring your group to see whether they're engaged, apathetic, clear, or confused—and adapting what you say, in real time, based on their expressions.

3. Give yourself home-field advantage.

Why do most sports teams have better records at home than they do away? Because we feel safe in familiar surroundings and can relax and give full attention to our performance.

That's not the case on the road. We are wired for "fight or flight" in new surroundings. We're distracted as we're monitoring our unfamiliar surroundings to see if we're in danger or at risk.

That's why it's in your best interest to familiarize yourself with the location of your interaction before the "real thing." For example, when I'm keynoting a conference, I always check out the hotel ballroom when no one's around (even if that's the previous night). I take the stage, throw my voice to the back of the room, and practice my opening at full volume.

Why is that important? Football coach Pop Warner said, "You play the way you practice." You can't practice at 50 percent and expect to be 100 percent in the real thing. Practicing the *way* you want to play, *where* you're going to play, means you've "been there, done that" so you can focus and give your full attention to connecting with your audience instead of feeling uncomfortable.

4. Tower, don't cower.

If you look meek and weak, you'll feel meek and weak. That's a problem because decision-makers don't respect people who don't command respect.

Unfortunately, that's what happened to a speaker who lost her audience at hello. The opening program started with Jim Collins (*Good to Great*) and then segued into Tom Peters (*In Search of Excellence*) and Seth Godin (*Linchpin*). We were all on the edge of our seats.

The next keynoter took center stage (good for her for getting out from behind the lectern), but then stood with her feet together, her head tucked down, and her hands in the dreaded fig leaf position. She said in a sing-songy voice, "I was telling my granddaughters yesterday how much I was looking forward to this...."

Within seconds, the digital devices came out and people started walking out. Which was a shame because, once she got going, she had valuable insights to share about her company's role in helping victims of 9/11. Unfortunately, her "cower" posture led people to conclude she wasn't worth listening to, and they didn't stay around to hear her program.

If you want to capture and keep people's attention, it's important to project a leadership presence that says, "I know what I'm talking about.

You can trust me to add value." You can do that by adopting the "I'm ready for anything" posture athletes assume when playing their sport. You can probably picture it. They have their:

- Feet shoulder-width apart so they're balanced and grounded
- Knees slightly bent so they're flexible and can move easily in any direction
- Head and chin up and eyes focused forward
- Hands centered in front, about a foot apart, like they're holding a basketball

Try it right now. Stand up, put your feet shoulder-width apart, bend your knees, pick your chin up, have basketball hands. That's the tower posture. Now, adopt the cower posture of the speaker who lost her audience. Put your:

- Feet close together. Do you feel unbalanced, "tipsy," like you're a pushover?
- Knees locked tight. Do you feel rigid, uptight, inflexible?
- Head down. Do you feel shy, coy, disconnected from your audience?
- Hands in the fig leaf position. Do you feel awkward, like you have something to hide?

Feel the difference? Choosing to tower, instead of cower, can help you command attention and respect. And in case you're wondering, yes, you can tower while sitting in an interview, meeting, or business meal. Just lift those shoulders, roll them back, and sit tall instead of slouching or slumping. There, doesn't that feel better? You will feel and look more confident and command more confidence from decision-makers when you choose to tower instead of cower.

Create Your Own Confidence Ritual

When you play under pressure every day, your rituals
keep you 100 percent focused on what you're doing.
WIMBLEDON CHAMPION TENNIS PLAYER RAFAEL NADAL

I'll always be grateful to two-time Grand Slam tennis champ "Rocket" Rod Laver for teaching me the importance of psyching myself *up* versus *out* with a personalized confidence ritual.

I had the privilege of comanaging Rod's tennis facility on Hilton Head Island in South Carolina. One day, he was gracious enough to ask if I wanted to hit some balls. Unfortunately, I was distracted with some logistics for a national tennis camp we were hosting the following week, and I was spraying balls all over the place. It was embarrassing. I finally said, "Rocket, I appreciate you rallying with me, but I'm wasting your time. We might as well quit."

Rocket looked at me and said, "The mark of a pro is the ability to turn around a bad day."

"But how do you do that?"

"You figure out the key part of your game and figure out a ritual around it. If the key to your game is getting your first serve in, you repeat 'first serve in' and give that all your attention. It gives you something to focus on instead of mentally being all over the map."

Rocket was right about the power of rituals. Does the name Pavlov ring a bell? Rituals are the secret to automatically focusing your attention on what you *do* want versus what you *don't* want.

Your goal is to create a confidence ritual you do religiously before every high-stakes communication. If you're a speaker, it may be saying, "I'm here to serve, not to shine; to make a difference, not to make a name" so you focus on what matters, which is connecting with and adding value to your audience. If you're interviewing for a job, it could be saying, "I'm going to find out and focus on what *their* needs are and how I can contribute to their organization" instead of "I've been out of work for ten months. *I need this job.*"

Author Seth Godin says, "Anxiety is experiencing failure in advance." By seeing communication as a sport and creating a confidence ritual, you can psych yourself up versus out so you look forward to this interaction instead of filling yourself with performance-compromising anxiety.

Action Questions:
Psych Yourself Up, Not Out

You have to believe in yourself when no one else does. That makes you a winner right there.

TENNIS PLAYER VENUS WILLIAMS

1. Please get out your W5 Form. What confidence ritual are you going to create and commit to doing before high-stakes communication so you psych yourself up versus out?

2. How are you going to see communication as a sport and prepare for an upcoming situation like you would for an important game or match? When and where are you going for a walk-and-rehearse so you can get good at thinking on your feet?

3. How will you physically or mentally familiarize yourself with the venue in advance to give yourself home-field advantage? How will you tower versus cower to project an "I'm ready for anything" leadership presence that commands attention and respect?

Part II

INTRIGUE

N = NEW

It's Not Enough to Be True; It Needs to Be NEW

*The world always seems brighter when you just
made something that wasn't there before.*

AUTHOR NEIL GAIMAN

The premise of this section is: just because something is important doesn't make it intriguing.

If you want busy, distracted people to give you their attention, it's important to, as Neil Gaiman points out, introduce something new, something that "wasn't there before."

Are you thinking, *Well, that's a problem because there's nothing new under the sun.*

Of course there is.

In fact, this section shows a variety of ways to produce and introduce fresh, first-of-their-kind ideas, approaches, and offerings that capture people's favorable attention because they're not only true, they're *new.*

Chapter 6

Create the Next New Thing

The only danger is not to evolve.

ENTREPRENEUR JEFF BEZOS

A special double issue of *Vanity Fair* magazine entitled "How the Web Was Won" featured interviews with online icons about the early days of the Internet. In that issue, Jeff Bezos revealed that Amazon was successful from the start despite naysayers who predicted failure. In fact, they were quickly backlogged with orders, so Jeff and a fellow executive headed to the shipping room to help process orders. They were on their hands and knees, packing up books, when his colleague turned to him and said, "This is really killing my knees and my back."

Jeff mulled it over, then said, "We should get kneepads."

His friend looked at him like he was crazy. "No Jeff, *we should get packing tables.*"[8]

What a great example of how intriguing it is when someone bypasses a "low hanging fruit" answer and introduces a more innovative, evolved way to solve a problem.

That's the point of this chapter. How can you disrupt the norm and think up new ideas and uncommon approaches and offerings so you break out instead of blend in?

Command Attention with Uncommon Approaches

When you can do the common things in life in an uncommon way, you will command the attention of the world.
INVENTOR GEORGE WASHINGTON CARVER

Are you thinking, *I agree in theory that people are intrigued by uncommon ideas, approaches, and offerings but how can I come up with them?*

The Seven Ps of Disruption are your tool for disrupting the norm in whatever you're doing and creating a next new thing that attracts the attention of your decision-makers. It doesn't matter whether you're starting a business, writing a blog, running a political campaign, or launching a product. If it's same-old, same-old, why should people pay attention?

Here's an example of how someone used the Seven Ps to create something original that created mutually rewarding connections for all involved.

How the Seven Ps of Disruption Can Help You Create a New Norm

You've got to be original. If you're like everybody else, what do they need you for?
ACTRESS BERNADETTE PETERS

The head of the healthcare division of an international Six Sigma training firm hired me to help him prepare for a Harvard medical conference. I asked him, "What's your purpose?"

He said, "This conference attracts hospital executives from around the world. If I do a good job, it could mean millions of dollars of new contracts for our company. The problem is, I'm speaking on the last day. I'm afraid no one's going to come to my program, much less sit through the whole thing and stay after to talk with me."

It's Not Enough to Be True; It Needs to Be NEW

"Got it. Let's use the Seven Ps to develop something so original and intriguing that it helps you optimize this opportunity."

1. First P = Purpose. What is your goal? What will make this a success?

"My purpose is to design and deliver a unique program that motivates people to show up and that delivers so much real-world value that everyone is favorably impressed," he told me.

2. P = Person. Who is your target decision-maker? Who represents your ideal client? Give this person a name. Describe him so you can see him.

"My target decision-maker is a seasoned hospital administrator, let's call him Gene, who has budget authority over ten medical centers," the client explained. "He is a little jaded because he's been to dozens of medical conferences and he's 'been there, heard that.'"

3. P = Problem. What frustrations/challenges does your target customer have?

"Well, at Six Sigma, we believe inefficiencies undermine performance, productivity, and profits in healthcare organizations. That's a problem Gene is facing on the job, and at this conference the problem is, Gene finds many medical presentations dense, dull, or too basic," the executive shared with me.

4. P = Premise. Ask "Why?" and "What if?" Why does it have to be that way? What if there were a new way, a better way?

"*What if* I could motivate Gene and other executives to stay for my program because it caught their eye and looked really intriguing?" he asked. "What if, instead of boring him with things he already knew, I delivered an innovative, substantive session that was fun and full of real-world actions he and his team could take to improve patient satisfaction, loyalty, and bottom-line profits?"

5. P = Product? This is where your brainstorming pays off with a new, better way. Asking "Why?" and "What if?" disrupts the SOP and yields a "Eureka! I have found it" product (or approach) that is more effective, appealing, rewarding, and profitable.

I asked my client, "What do you do in your spare time? Do you have any hobbies?"

He laughed ruefully, "I'm on the road for days a week. Who has time for hobbies?"

"How about when you're home? Do you and your wife like movies, like to garden, watch TV?"

"We watch *Law and Order* sometimes."

"Bingo. I've got your intriguing title for you . . . FLAW AND ORDER."

He laughed. "That's perfect."

We developed his program so it played like a plot of the TV show. He identified three *flaws* costing hospitals profits and prescribed how to set up Six Sigma systems to bring *order* to the chaos to improve employee productivity and to increase patient satisfaction, loyalty, and revenue.

6. P = Promise. Because this is new, make a promise so people can trust it and you.

My client said, "Our description promises this will be innovative, interactive, unlike anything they've experienced at a medical conference and that it will also deliver pragmatic recommendations that can boost their bottom line so they can trust there will be a financial payoff."

7. P = POP. Give your new product an intriguing name that will pop it out of its pack.

My client said, "I really do think the title *Flaw and Order* will motivate people to stay around for my session on the final day and choose to attend my program instead of the other breakouts."

He was right. His new offering filled the room, resulted in excellent evaluations, and motivated a number of participants to voluntarily approach him (without him pitching from the platform) and ask for his card so they could have a follow-up conversation.

The Benefits of Creating Something New

When you create, you get a little endorphin rush. Why do you think Einstein's hair looked like that?

COMEDIAN ROBIN WILLIAMS

When you create a new, better approach, you're not the only one who gets an endorphin rush. Your customers get an endorphin rush of intrigued attention and you get a rush of new business.

How about you? Get out your W5 Form. In fact, I suggest you take it, these Seven Ps, and a friend to lunch. Divide up the time so each of you can brainstorm a priority. Talk through the Seven Ps and ask "Why?" and "What if?" so each of you can disrupt the SOP and create a new norm that will attract the favorable attention of your decision-makers.

Want one more example of the bottom-line benefits that can accrue to you and who you want to connect with when you use the Seven Ps to create something new?

I was in downtown New York at rush hour and needed to get to the airport. Even though I was in the street scanning for cabs, I wasn't able to find one. I called my son Andrew. "Help?"

He said, "Mom, I'll take care of it. Where are you?" Five minutes later, a cab pulled up, I jumped in, and made my flight on time. Andrew had even prepaid the fare. Such a deal.

You may have guessed the "evolutionary" company I'm talking about. Ladies and gentlemen, meet Uber. According to the *New York*

Times, Uber started less than five years ago and has already expanded to 128 locations worldwide and received a *Forbes* estimated valuation of $18.2 billion in 2014.[9]

How the Seven Ps Can Help You Create Happy Customers

No business has ever failed with happy customers.
BILLIONAIRE WARREN BUFFETT

I didn't consult with Uber, but we can have fun imagining and reverse-engineering how they created the next new thing in a multibillion-dollar industry. Imagine you're an executive in the beginning days of Uber, brainstorming with the Seven Ps.

1. P = Purpose.

Our goal is to give millions of unhappy people a new, better way to get a cab. Our objective is to create a competitive edge, corner a niche, and build a profitable business.

2. P = Person.

Our target customer is a successful professional, let's call her Judy, who lives or works in a major city, and she's tired of trying to flag down cabs.

3. P = Problem.

The problems Judy has with taxis are . . .

- ◆ It's impossible to get a cab in rush hour, when it's raining, or in the middle of winter
- ◆ Drivers often overcharge, and there's nothing you can do about it
- ◆ Cabs often reek of cigarette smoke; seats are dirty and ruin her clothes

- Many drivers prefer cash and don't want her to pay with a credit card

4. P = Premise.

Our premise is there's got to be a new, better way to get a taxi.

- What if Judy could get a cab at any hour and never had to wait more than fifteen minutes?
- What if, even when it was rush hour or raining, Judy could count on getting a cab?
- What if Judy could trust her driver had GPS and knew how to get to her destination?
- What if the fee was paid in advance with her credit card so Judy never had to carry cash?
- What if all cabs were inspected so Judy could trust them to be clean and smoke-free?

5. P = Product.

We have a new, better taxi company that gives frustrated taxi-seekers exactly what they do want and nothing of what they don't want.

6. P = Promise.

We're going to gain Judy's trust, and the trust of other skeptical first-timers, by offering an initial money-back guarantee so there's no risk and they don't have anything to lose.

7. P = POP.

Let's pick an easy-to-pronounce-and-remember name that helps it go viral.

How Are You Different?

If you're lucky enough to be different, don't ever change.

SINGER TAYLOR SWIFT

See what can happen when you take the time to apply the Seven Ps to your priority? If you want happy customers, give them what they want and nothing of what they don't want. That may seem like it's common sense, but as my mom used to say, "Just because something is common sense, doesn't mean it's common practice."

How about you? Is your idea or organization not getting the support, traction, or revenue it deserves? Maybe people see it as nothing special. If they consider it a commodity, they have no compelling reason to pay attention to it. Unless you're perceived as different, you'll always struggle for attention. The good news is, the Seven Ps can help you create something new so you're not just leading the crowd; you've created a brand new crowd.

Action Questions: Create the Next New Thing

Every business is successful exactly to the extent it does something others cannot.

PAYPAL COFOUNDER PETER THIEL

1. Look at your W5 Form. What are the norms in that industry? What is standard operating procedure in the issue you're addressing? How are things always done in that situation?

2. How will you use the Seven Ps of Disruption to identify a new, better way to solve that problem, approach that issue, meet that need?

3. How do you plan to attract the attention (and business) of your target customers by introducing something uncommon, by offering something your competitors cannot?

Chapter 7

Keep Current

If you learn to like being a beginner, the whole world opens up to you.
AUTHOR BARBARA SHER

The speaker before me at a global young entrepreneur conference was an advertising legend who had founded a top agency in New York City. He launched into his keynote with a story about Hall of Fame jockey Eddie Arcaro, who won two horseracing Triple Crowns more than seventy years ago. He then referenced World War II, quoted General George Patton, and told the often-used "motivational" story about how elephants are trained with a chain around their leg until they stop trying to break free and you can tie them up with a shoestring. Hmmm.

I looked around. No one was listening. These students weren't being rude; they just couldn't relate to anything he was saying. Not only did all his references occur before they were born; they were US-centric. He either hadn't asked himself if his remarks were current or didn't care.

Please note: I'm not disrespecting this individual's contributions to his industry. It's just that there was an easy fix. If he had spent even a few minutes researching his group, he would have discovered they were all in their late teens and early twenties. He could have made his talk more topical by holding up a newspaper (props!) that dissected the top ads at the Super Bowl, which had taken place the previous weekend. He could have asked the students their opinions of which ads worked, which didn't, and why.

He could have asked attendees how they were advertising *their* businesses and offered advice on to how to stretch their marketing dollars. Either of these options would have served his audience and made his expertise current. Instead of being willing to be a "beginner," he elected to give the same talk he'd been giving for years. As a result, his remarks fell on uninterested ears.

Are You Citing Recent Resources?

When it comes to speaking engagements, I don't read prepared speeches. I don't want to do the same thing over and over.
DANNY MEYER, FOUNDER OF THREE MICHELIN STAR RESTAURANTS

How about you? Do you give the same talk over and over? Do you read prepared speeches, verbatim? Do you cite outdated research and resources?

Part of INTRIGUE is understanding people don't want to hear the same thing over and over. *Recency equals relevancy.* To the degree you're current is to the degree that you're cutting edge. Think about it. Why do we read or watch the news? We have an innate curiosity about current affairs. We want to stay up-to-date about what's new in the world around us.

Yet many of us use outdated resources and research. As soon as we do, people roll their eyes and conclude we're out of date.

This was an eye-opener for an executive who brought an outline of his leadership book to our first coaching session. I noticed he had started every chapter with a quote. As you may have noticed, I love quotes. I think they serve many positive purposes. Pithy, provocative quotes break up dense content so it's more visually appealing and can pop off the page and get eyebrows up.

The challenge was, all (and I mean all) of my client's quotes were from what my millennial friends call "dead white guys." Now, I like Einstein, Aristotle, Edison, and Emerson as much as the next person. It's not that these thought leaders weren't wise; they're just not recent.

I told him, "Want a quick way to make your book more intriguing? Replace some of these old quotes with new quotes your readers won't have seen before."

"But I like those quotes."

"I know, a lot of people like those quotes. And that's a problem. People often scan a book to see if it's worth reading. If they see several quotes they already know, they put the book back because they conclude it doesn't have anything *new* to offer."

"So what can I do?"

"It's easy. You're writing about leadership. All you have to do is enter 'quotes on leadership' into your favorite search engine. Up will come Brainy Quotes, Think Exist, Goodreads, and other quote aggregators that offer a variety of free quotes on your subject."

We jumped online and quickly found several quotes that were perfect lead-ins for his chapters. In fact, he announced this one from business author Ken Blanchard had become his new favorite: "The key to successful leadership today is influence, not authority."

Quotes from Today's Thought Leaders Are an Easy Way to Be Current

Remind yourself this moment is the only one you know you have for sure.

ENTREPRENEUR OPRAH WINFREY

Would you like to find quotes from today's thought leaders that capture your people's positive attention? Just put "quotes on _____ (your topic)" into a quote aggregator. Review the quotes that come up with these criteria in mind to find just the right ones.

1. Which of these is most relevant to my audience, topic, and the point I want to make?

2. Which offers provocative insights that stretch my thinking and offers fresh perspective?

3. Which quotes represent a diverse mix of men and women and a variety of leaders or pop icons of different ages, industries, cultures, and countries?

4. How I can offset "old" quotes ("Time is the coin of your life … Be careful lest you let others spend it for you."—Carl Sandburg); with new quotes ("Time is the new money"—Richard Branson)?

5. How can I "hook and hinge" this quote to my content so it supports my point? For example, if you quote Mitch Albom's "I'm in love with hope," you could take the key words *love* or *hope* and ask "What are you in love with?" or "What do you hope for?"

In case you're interested, our Intrigue Agency team keeps an updated list of our favorite top one hundred current quotes. You're welcome to request a copy by contacting us at the email address at the end of this book.

Associate with Current Events Your Customers Care About

Creative people are able to connect experiences and synthesize new things.

STEVE JOBS

A workshop participant said, "I own an accounting firm. Nothing very intriguing, new, or current about that. Any suggestions on how to get more attention for my business?"

I suggested, "You might want to follow the example of Quicken Loans. They got national attention by linking to March Madness, the hugely popular NCAA college basketball tournament that is followed by millions of fans. They sponsored a contest that promised one *billion* dollars to anyone who selected the winner of every game. A *USA Today* article by Bruce Horovitz said this novel partnership increased Quicken Loans's brand awareness by a whopping 300 percent in one month.[10] *That's* brand attention."

"Yes it is, but I don't have a billion dollars to spend on a marketing campaign or prize money."

I told her, "You don't have to; just look for current events that are *already* generating press. Instead of trying to build interest from scratch, connect with something that's got built-in buzz."

I suggested to her (and to you) that you can come to the attention of potential customers by linking to current events they're already paying attention to. For example:

◆ What holidays or annual events could you leverage? What natural tie-ins might you have with April 15 tax prep? Graduation? Thanksgiving? Valentine's Day?

◆ What activities are popular in your community? Fishing tournament? Farmers' market? County fair? Could you sponsor them, have a booth at them?

◆ What causes are getting press in your local media? Dress for Success Clothing Drive? Humane Society Bark Park and Pet-working Gala? Save the River 10K?

I told the accountant, "Denny's [the restaurant chain] gets free press every year by serving free meals to military vets on Veterans Day. Perhaps you could do something similar and offer a free financial seminar for the veterans in your area on Veterans Day. When you link with current activities potential customers care about, they're more likely to care about you."

She told me, "You know what I'm going to do? I have two grand-kids who play Little League, and my son runs a pizza parlor in town. I'm going to sponsor an all-expenses-paid pizza party for the winning team at his restaurant."

I told her, "That's smart. You're contributing to your community in a way that is in alignment with your priorities *and* you're putting yourself on the radar of potential clients who might not be aware of you otherwise. Sounds like a win all the way around to me."

Offer Commentary on What's Current

I always had a running commentary in my head that
was extremely funny, but I never said it to anyone.
COMEDIAN ELAYNE BOOSLER

In today's world of social media, you don't even have to leave your home to connect your priority with current events. You can do it by getting your commentary out of your head and offering enlightening insight to what's current online.

That's what Jeffrey Ritter, attorney and cybersecurity consultant, did as a result of attending one of our strategic retreats. He told us, "As an executive at a law firm, I was flown around the globe to speak at conferences on digital trust. I expected that to continue when I started my own consulting practice. Unfortunately, it hasn't worked out that way. How can I get more clients?"

I said, "Jeffrey, you're in luck. You have a perfect opportunity coming up to get worldwide attention for your work, for free."

"That sounds too good to be true. How?"

"The Olympics are next month. Don't they depend on digital trust? I mean, we have to trust the electronic cameras and digital clocks are accurate and telling the truth, right? You can follow the games' most popular hashtags on social media and post about the events getting the most traffic."

Jeffrey acted on that advice. As a result of the media attention (and respect) he generated, he was hired as a professor at Georgetown, Johns Hopkins, and *Oxford*. Not too shabby. Without leaving home, Jeffrey brought his work to the attention of millions by commenting on what was current.

Put this in perspective. Blogs, articles, videos, and posts filled with how-to's and expert advice will be read, maybe, by relatives and a few dedicated individuals interested in your topic.

A better way to get your work noticed by more people is to add intriguing commentary to current events your ideal customers are already paying attention to. By linking to high-profile events, you can jump on their bandwagon of buzz and come to the attention of people who might not otherwise know about, or care about, you and your offering.

Action Questions: Keep Current

We don't write about something unless we have something new to add.
COAUTHORS OF *FREAKONOMICS*
STEVE LEVITT AND STEPHEN DUBNER

1. How will you keep current? How will you quote current resources and cite recent research so you have something new to add to the situation identified on your W5 Form?

2. How will you offer commentary on current events to jump on the bandwagon of buzz and attention they're already generating instead of having to create your own from scratch?

3. If your priority isn't new, how can you link it to something that is? How will you connect with ideal customers who aren't aware of you by linking with a current event they care about?

Chapter 8

Look at the World with Reawakened Eyes

*When the eye wakes up to see again, it suddenly
stops taking anything for granted.*

PHILOSOPHER FREDERICK FRANCK

I remember reading this article in the *Washington Post Magazine*, Sunday edition, blogging about it afterward and thinking to myself, *Just give the man the Pulitzer.*

Gene Weingarten's "Pearls before Breakfast"[11] was such a brilliant piece of journalism. He wondered, "What would happen if you took a renowned violinist (whose latest album was called "unfailingly exquisite, a musical summit that will make your heart thump and weep at the same time") and positioned him inside a DC metro stop during the morning commute?

What if you asked him to play six compositions, each "masterpieces that have endured for centuries on their brilliance alone"? What if you took this experiment one step further and asked him to play these musical works of art on a rare, multimillion-dollar Stradivarius?

Would any of the hundreds of people streaming by take a moment to pay attention to a free concert by "one of the finest classical musicians in the world, playing some of the most elegant music ever written on one of the most valuable violins ever made"?

In the forty-five minutes Joshua Bell played (yes, *the* Joshua Bell, who packs them in at concert halls around the globe), only seven (!) people paid any attention to his performance. The other 1,070 people all rushed by, seemingly oblivious to the miracle in their midst.

Weingarten's point? There were several. One of which was to quote W. H. Davies, who said, " 'What is this life if, full of care, we have no time to stop and stare.' At what cost are we so busy, so driven, we have lost the ability to see, hear, and be grateful for the beauty around us?"

Another intriguing insight, "There was no demographic pattern to distinguish the few people who stopped to watch Bell from the majority who hurried past. But *every time a child walked past, he or she tried to stop and watch. And every single time, a parent scooted the kid away.*"

Makes you think, doesn't it? Kudos to Gene Weingarten for his brilliant writing and thought-provoking social experiment. Please take the time to read his article and then ask, "Would I have taken a moment to listen to Bell? Why or why not? Have I become so busy, so preoccupied, I've become inured to my surroundings? Am I missing the miracles around me? At what cost?

Are You Paying Attention to the Miracles in Your Midst?

Perhaps we never really appreciate the here and now until it is challenged.

AVIATOR ANNE MORROW LINDBERGH

I included this chapter because I've come to understand that part of INTRIGUE is vowing to see the world with new, fresh (versus old, tired) eyes. You may agree it's important to pay attention to the miracles in our midst instead of taking them for granted, yet that's what many of us do.

Why? If you studied Maslow's hierarchy of needs, you may remember one of its premises is "a satisfied need is no longer a motivator." What does that mean? If we have freedom, money, health, work, friends, and family, those are "satisfied needs," so we stop paying attention to them.

In fact, we tend to take things for granted until we have an SEE—a significant emotional event. Unfortunately, most SEEs are traumatic. We get divorced, fired, sick, or lose a loved one.

Why wait for a painful SEE to focus your attention on what really matters? Why not have a pretend SEE so you can get the epiphany without the pain? Why not choose to override Maslow's hierarchy of needs and reconnect with who and what's important, starting today?

Two Ways to Reconnect with Who and What's Important

The moment one gives close attention to anything, even a blade of grass, it becomes a mysterious, awesome, indescribably magnificent world in itself.

PLAYWRIGHT HENRY MILLER

Are you thinking, "But how can we override Maslow's hierarchy of needs?" Here's how. These two ways can help you pay closer attention to who and what really matter.

1. See someone or something as if for the first time

He who can no longer pause to wonder and stand rapt in awe, is as good as dead, his eyes are closed.

GENIUS ALBERT EINSTEIN

My sons and I had a nightly bedtime ritual while they were growing up. They would say their "thankfuls" and I would tell a story while giving them a backrub. We had made up playful names for the different types: "slap happy, finger rain, electricity, and chop suey."

One night, I was sitting right next to them, giving them a "bumper-car" backrub, but I wasn't really paying attention. I was flying out the next morning to give a workshop and was preoccupied with, "Did I pack my handouts? Is there gas in the car? What time's the flight?"

Then, for some reason, my eyes settled on Tom and Andrew. I *saw* them as if for the first or last time. An ordinary moment became an extraordinary moment. I was filled with the sheer miracle of their youth, vitality, bright-eyed curiosity, robust health. I was flooded with how fortunate I was to be their mom, to have them in my life and to be in theirs.

Author Doris Lessing said, "It's all a matter of keeping my eyes open." You can turn ordinary moments into extraordinary moments anytime you want. Simply put aside what you're doing, look around, and *see* someone or something as if for the first or last time. As soon as you do, you'll see that person with renewed appreciation because you're seeing him or her with intrigued eyes.

2. Ink it when you think it

"The horror of that moment," the King went on, "I shall never, NEVER forget!"
"You will, though," the Queen said, "If you don't make a memorandum of it."

AUTHOR LEWIS CARROLL

Did you read *Alice in Wonderland*? Do you remember the above passage? Even the Queen knew to jot thoughts when they're hot.

I'll always be grateful to former *National Geographic* photographer Dewitt Jones for showing me why it's so important to ink it when we think it. Dewitt and I were enjoying a walk/talk along a Maui beach discussing the topic of intuition. What is intuition? Where does it come from? Why are those intuitive nudges never wrong? How can we capitalize on them?

Dewitt was doing something that puzzled me. We'd go about one hundred yards and Dewitt would stop, whip out a little notebook and pen from his pocket, and write something down. We'd go another couple hundred yards and Dewitt would stop and scribble something else down. He kept doing this until I finally asked, "Dewitt, what are you doing?"

He said, "Sam, I'd get ideas and think, 'That'd be an interesting tidbit for my column' or 'I've got to include that in my keynote,' but then I'd get caught up in other things and forget them. I realized I make my living from my mind, and I was throwing away these golden insights that were being gifted to me. I promised myself I'd start writing them down the moment they occurred to me so I wouldn't lose them. Now, it's become a habit."

How many times have you noticed or thought of something intriguing and then gone about your day and forgotten it? If there's anything I've learned in years of researching the fascinating topics of innovation and INTRIGUE, it's that *this* is how our best thoughts occur. They pop into our mind. And if we don't write them down in the moment, they disappear and get drowned out by other things competing for our attention.

From now on, promise you'll "take note" of those flashes of brilliance. Carry a notebook or digital recorder, or call yourself on your phone and leave a message. Do something to capture intriguing observations before they disappear. Remember, they don't call 'em fleeting thoughts for nothing.

Jotting down thoughts when they're hot is my modus operandi. I hope it becomes yours. I can hardly express how big of a difference it will make if you make your life your lab and ink it when you think it.

Author Natalie Goldberg says, "Writers get to live life twice." If you ink it when you think it, you get to live life *thrice*. Once in real time when you observe something intriguing and write it down. A second time when you review your notes and recall that flash of inspiration. A third time when your share your intriguing insight and witness it making a difference for others.

What Are You Giving Your Attention To?

Tell me to what you're paying attention and I'll tell you who you are.
PHILOSOPHER JOSÉ ORTEGA Y GASSET

Starting today, vow to take note of what's right with your world instead of what's wrong. Instead of focusing attention on the *news*, which dwells on man's inhumanity to man, deliberately choose to give your attention to what's uplifting. For example, watch Eric Whitacre conduct a "virtual choir" with two thousand people from fifty-eight countries ... all at the same time, *online*.[12]

As author Dr. Wayne Dyer says, "When you change the way you look at things, the things you look at change. By paying closer attention to who and what really matters, you'll start appreciating the miracle of the mundane. Focusing on what's right will help you see your life in a new light.

Action Questions: See the World with Reawakened Eyes

The real voyage of discovery consists not of seeking new landscapes, but in having new eyes.
AUTHOR MARCEL PROUST

1. Who will you reconnect with by seeing that person with new versus tired eyes? How will you make it a daily habit to see someone or something as if for the first or last time?

2. How are you going to override Maslow's hierarchy of needs and pay closer attention to who and what really matters, today and every day?

3. How will you jot down thoughts and ink it when you think it so you take note of what's right with the world versus what's wrong?

Chapter 9

Cause Aha's with Ha-Ha's

It has always surprised me how little attention philosophers have paid to humor, since it is a more significant process of mind than reason. Reason can only sort out perceptions, but humor can change them.

AUTHOR EDWARD DE BONO

Smart man, that Edward de Bono. Humor (ha-ha's) not only has the power to capture people's favorable attention, but it can produce epiphanies (aha's) by helping them see things in new ways.

Is there any surer sign you've got people's favorable attention than when they're laughing? As comedian Joan Rivers said, "When you're laughing at something, you remember something."

One client told me, "I know humor is important, but I'm not funny."

I said, "You may think you're not funny, but everyone has funny things happen to and around them. All you have to do is start noticing things that make you laugh and hook and hinge them (with attribution) to your topic.

They Don't Call It Comic Relief for Nothing

If you don't take yourself too seriously, pretty soon, you find the humor in everyday life. And sometimes, it can be a lifesaver.

ACTRESS BETTY WHITE

Is the situation on your W5 Form "serious business"? Do you assume you need to stay serious if it's a serious topic? Wrong. People can pay attention to serious stuff for only so long. They may understand they're *supposed* to listen, but if it requires discipline, incentive, or bandwidth they don't have, what you're saying will not get through.

That's where a good laugh comes in. Appropriate humor gives people a mental break from the hard work of trying to stay focused. A smile or laugh restarts people's attention span.

I better practice what I teach. I've just spent a page *explaining* the benefits of humor. Why not share an example that shows how you can create an aha with a ha-ha?

How to Integrate True Humor into Your Interactions

I learned at an early age that when I made people laugh,
they liked me. This is a lesson I never forgot.

HUMOR COLUMNIST ART BUCHWALD

Years ago while I was in the San Francisco airport, a very tall man was walking toward me from the opposite direction. I couldn't believe it. Some people in front of me were pointing at him and laughing. I thought, *How rude, there's no excuse for that.*

When he got closer, I could see why they were laughing. He had on a t-shirt that said in large letters, "No, I'm NOT a basketball player." As he went by, I turned to say something and burst out laughing. The back of his t-shirt read, "Are you a jockey?"

I had to meet this clever young man, so I raced back to catch up with him. I asked, "Where'd you get that terrific t-shirt?"

He smiled and said, "This is nothing. I've got a whole drawer full of these at home. My favorite one says, 'I'm 6'13" and the weather up here is fine.'"

I asked, "How did you come up with these?"

"Oh, I didn't come up with them. My mom did. I grew a foot between the time I was sixteen and eighteen years old. I didn't even want to go outside because everyone had to make a smart aleck remark. My mom finally told me, 'If you can't beat 'em, join 'em.' She's the one who thought these up. Now I have fun *with* my height instead of being frustrated *by* my height."

What a wonderful example of how humor can be a saving grace. Instead of taking himself too seriously, that smart young man came up with a comeback and lightened up versus tightened up.

Hook and Hinge Punchlines to Your Point

It's a privilege to be in people's homes, but I'm on so late
I'm definitely the last seconds of anyone's attention. I
just want to give them something to laugh at.

TONIGHT SHOW HOST JIMMY FALLON

After sharing a humorous story, be sure to "hook and hinge" the punchline back to your audience so it's relevant for them. The "hook" is the key phrase or point of your story. In this case, the hook is "having fun with it instead of being frustrated by it." "Hinge" that phrase back to your audience with a "you question" so they can think about how this might apply to them.

For example, you could ask, "Are you sensitive or self-conscious about something? Would you like to have fun with it instead of being frustrated by it? Why not come up with a noncombative comeback so you can be amused with, rather than annoyed by, that situation?"

Another teaching moment from that encounter in the airport? As soon as it happened, I *knew* it was humor gold, and I would somehow share it in my programs and books. From now on, understand that the funny things that happen to or around you are a gift. Unwrap them. Identify the lesson learned and hook and hinge it into a relevant communication so that ha-ha produces an aha.

A client told me, "I'm not comfortable telling jokes. Most of the jokes I hear either fall flat or I find them offensive. I don't want to risk alienating my audience."

I told him, "I'm glad you brought that up. I agree it's unwise to tell jokes. Jokes are polarizing, plus they're 'made up.' I'm suggesting you use *true* humor so people can trust you. When you share real-life experiences, you maintain credibility because you're not fabricating things."

Look for What Makes You Laugh Out Loud

Humor is everywhere in that there is irony in
just about everything a human does.
BILL NYE, THE SCIENCE GUY

At the midnight hour, during Denise Brosseau's final read-through of her "Ready to Be a Thought Leader?" manuscript, she realized it was a bit too serious and would be more intriguing if she added some true humor. All she had to do was think about situations that had made her laugh out loud in the recent past and tie them in to her material.

For example, one of her chapters discussed her view that advanced degrees are nice, but not necessary to be considered a thought-leader in your field. To illustrate that point, she shared what happened while shopping at a Babies "R" Us store near Stanford University.

While waiting to check out, she was entertained by a couple in front of her who were warily reading the instructions on the box that said the crib they were about to buy had to be assembled from scratch. They nervously asked the cashier, "Will we be able to put this together ourselves?"

The casher asked innocently, "Do you have college degrees?"

"Oh, yes," the man assured her, "I have an MBA and my wife has a PhD."

The cashier flashed a big smile, "Then you're going to need to hire someone." Bada boom.

Denise told me, "The cashier's response was so unexpected, we all cracked up. I weave that story into my presentations now, and it always gets a big laugh."

Denise is right. Unexpected responses usually do elicit laughs. In fact, do you know how Einstein knew he had a good idea? He laughed out loud. That's why it's in your best interests to keep your antennae up for irony, defined as an "unexpected outcome."

From now on, when something unexpected causes you to laugh, write it down. Then figure out how you can integrate it into an upcoming situation to give people a respite from the "serious stuff" and to restart their positive attention for you and your topic.

Where Else Can You Find Appropriate Humor?

If you can get humor and seriousness at the same time,
you've created a special thing. That's what I'm looking for,
because if you get pompous, you lose everything.
SINGER PAUL SIMON

Where else can you find true humor? Believe it or not, I never read the *Wall Street Journal* or the *Washington Post* without finding an intriguing insight or laugh-out-loud anecdote that can add a humorous punch to a point I want to make.

A story in the *Washington Post* about former Congresswoman Pat Schroeder (D–CO) illustrates this perfectly. When Schroeder first arrived at her office in the Rayburn Building, she was surprised to find a gift waiting for her from a renowned prankster, Charlie Wilson (D–TX).

Schroeder opened it up with great anticipation, only to find a picture of a tombstone with the inscription, "Here lies Davy Crockett's wife." Underneath it, Wilson had scribbled a note, "In Texas, women don't even rate their own headstone."[13]

The nerve! She marched down the hall to his office, ready to give him a piece of her mind. She stormed into his office, only to discover him leaning back in his chair with his cowboy boots up on his desk. Wilson greeted her with a big grin and said, "Hey there, Babycakes."

Schroeder realized she had a choice. She could read him the riot act, but what purpose would that serve? Instead she fired back, "That's Congresswoman Babycakes to you."

Wilson laughed, they became friends, and ended up cosponsoring legislation together.

Now, you may be thinking, *Why didn't Schroeder unload on him?* She could have, but then Wilson would have continued teasing her because it *worked*. Instead, she gave as good as she got, which caused him to see her in a new light and they became allies instead of enemies.

I'm not suggesting you laugh off truly egregious behavior. There are times it's important to push back if you're being treated inappropriately. There are also times, as Pat Schroeder and the tall young man demonstrated, you can transform negative attention into positive attention with the saving grace of humor.

Action Questions: Turn Your Ha-Ha's into Aha's

If you can laugh at it. you can live with it.
HUMOR COLUMNIST ERMA BOMBECK

1. Think about the situation you've identified on your W5 Form. Could you lose people's attention if it's unrelentingly serious? How are you going to provide comic relief?

2. What's happened to or around you that made you laugh out loud? How can you hook and hinge that into your topic so people see your issue in new, more positive ways?

Part III

INTRIGUE

T = TIME-EFFICIENT

Win Trust by Being TIME-EFFICIENT

If you don't have anything to do, don't do it here.

OFFICE POSTER

A premise of INTRIGUE is that people are chronically impatient.

Their internal clock is always ticking.

We have to prove, and keep proving, we're a good use of their time and attention.

If we don't, they will mentally move on to something that is.

This section has a variety of ways to keep your interactions concise and to the point, so people can trust you will be time and attention well spent.

Chapter 10

Keep It Brief or They'll
Give You Grief

Let's address the elephant in the room. "YO Elephant!"

HUMORIST GENE WEINGARTEN

Do you know what the elephant in the room is in every business interaction? The underlying concern of "how long will this take?"

As a popular office poster says, "Opportunity knocks. People barge right in." If people barge in and don't ask if this is a good time, we become resentful and anxious.

Anxious? Yes, *anxiety* is defined as "not knowing." If we *don't know* how long someone wants our attention, *we don't* pay attention. We're thinking, *Don't you realize you're interrupting me? Hurry it up. I've got things to do.*

It's like the famous *New Yorker* cartoon from Bob Mankoff that shows an executive on the phone saying, "How about Tuesday. No? How about never? Is never good for you?"

From now on, if you want people to pay attention, preface your interaction by asking for a specific amount of their time, and pleasantly surprise them by asking for *less* time than expected.

The Secret to Motivating People to Give You Their Precious Attention

"We need a support group for non-stop talkers;
we're going to call it On and On Anon."

<small>COMEDIAN PAULA POUNDSTONE</small>

An entrepreneur told me he was on his way to England to pitch his app to the London Olympics' chief technology officer (CTO). I said, "What a great opportunity, Mike. How much time do you have?"

"One hour."

I said, "Want some unsolicited input? You can win buy-in by making the first words out of your mouth, 'I know we have an hour scheduled, and I also know you've got 212 days left to prepare for the games. I can only imagine how much you have on your plate. I've distilled my pitch into ten minutes. If you'd like to continue the conversation after that, I welcome it.'"

He said, "But that's not enough time to explain how my app works."

"Mike, that CTO is under so much pressure, if you take longer than ten minutes, he's not going to be paying attention, anyway. He may even be resenting you for keeping him from his other priorities. It's in your best interests to keep it brief so he *wants* to hear more."

Curious as to the rest of that story? The CTO did not contract for Mike's app, saying there wasn't enough ramp-up time to make it happen. He did, however, compliment Mike on his professionalism and told him he'd keep the door open for future business opportunities.

Which is the point. Taking less time than anticipated is no guarantee you'll get the business. It is a guarantee you're more likely to get people's favorable attention and goodwill.

How to Keep It Concise and Productive

*The simple act of paying positive attention to people
has a great deal to do with productivity.*

AUTHOR TOM PETERS

A company executive hired me to work with one of his project engineers. He told me, "Rick [not his real name] knows his stuff but he's a talker. It's like he's pathologically unable to get to the point. His meetings take three times longer than they need to. His team talks about him behind his back. This is compromising his career. Can you help him be more concise?"

I told the executive, "I agree this can be a career-maker or -breaker. The good news is, being time-efficient is a learnable skill. I look forward to working with him."

Half an hour into our first meeting, I understood the executive's concerns. It was clear to me that Rick was all over the map because he had no map. He just kept talking until he ran out of things to say. He never really asked himself if what he was saying was valuable or relevant.

Because he was an engineer, I anticipated he'd respect metrics, so we started applying numerical limits to his interactions. I told him, "Think about it. Twitter is 140 characters long. Not 141. 140. The message won't send if it's too long. That's the type of numerical accountability you want to attach to all your communications from now on."

Rick was smart and quickly came up with other examples of time and space boundaries. "Snapchats are eight seconds long. TED talks are eighteen minutes long. Vines are six seconds long. Seth Godin's blog is almost always under two hundred words."

"Exactly. And do you know about Five-Sentence Emails? They have a cut-and-paste statement you can put in your signature line to explain your policy of sending short emails. The average business worker sends 43 emails a day and receives 130, so keeping your emails brief can make a huge difference in whether people choose to pay attention to them."

People Pay More Attention when You're Succinct

I try to leave out the parts people skip.
AUTHOR ELMORE LEONARD

I told Rick, "The beauty of putting time and space limits on your communication is it holds you accountable for leaving out the parts people skip."

"But how do I know what to keep in and what to leave out?"

"Well, Guy Kawasaki, a big proponent of short emails, says you can balance succinctness with politeness by providing just enough information to answer these five questions:

- ◆ Who are you?
- ◆ What do you want?
- ◆ Why are you asking me?
- ◆ Why should I do what you're asking me?
- ◆ What is the next step?"

I asked Rick, "How about meetings? Do you have a time limit?"

"Not really. We take however long we need to get through our agenda and cover our objectives."

"Uh oh," I said. "You've heard of Parkinson's Law, which is, 'A task expands to the time allowed for it?' Horn's Law is 'Communications expand to the time allowed for them.' From now on, everyone in your meetings, including you, is going to have three minutes, max, to report out on each issue. That forces everyone to share only what's crucial for the group to know. People determine whether they can trust us based on whether we keep our time promises. So appoint a timekeeper and let everyone know we're all busy, so from now on, you can trust our meetings to start and end on time, and for everyone to be held accountable for their time limits."

Put a ThunderShirt on Your Communication

A deadline is negative inspiration. Still, it's better than no inspiration at all.

Rita Mae Brown

While Rick and I were talking about this, a rather impressive thunderstorm moved into our area. Lightning flashed in the distance, and my dog Murphy started pacing and panting. I said, "Excuse me, Rick, I need to put a ThunderShirt on Murphy. She gets panicked by these storms."

Rick watched while I Velcro'd Murph into her ThunderShirt. He asked, "How does that work?"

"Well, it's like swaddling a baby. Babies feel insecure when they flail around because the world seems endless. But when you wrap them snugly in a blanket, their world feels finite, safe, kind of like the womb. It works the same way with Murphy. As soon as she's swaddled in a ThunderShirt, her energy is contained and confined so she calms down."

Rick started laughing and said, "Sam, that's what we're doing. We're putting a ThunderShirt on my meetings and emails. We're swaddling my communication."

Swaddle Your Communication

When forced to work within a tight framework, the imagination is taxed to its utmost and produces its richest ideas. Given total freedom, the work is likely to sprawl.

POET T. S. ELLIOT

Rick and I had a fascinating conversation over lunch about his new commitment to "keeping it concise." Our discussion has had an enduring impact on me. If I'm "flailing around and all over the place," I realize my communication is open-ended and I need to swaddle it. Assigning snug deadlines and tighter space boundaries forces me to make "every word tell."

For example, I put a ten-page ThunderShirt on these chapters. That changed my editing mindset. The operative question was no longer "Is this an intriguing example or insight?" The question was "Am I over my ten-page limit? If so, something has to go."

The truth is, as important as something may seem, people don't miss it if we don't put it in.

It's been fun hearing how clients are running with this idea of swaddling their interactions. An association exec told me, "I can't wait to propose this to our board. We've had trouble getting volunteers for committees, and I think I know why. It's too much of a wide-open commitment. People don't want to agree to something when they don't know how much time it's going to take. Or they're tired of meetings where everyone spins their wheels and nothing gets done. I'm going to recommend we put a ThunderShirt on the time requirements. "If we promise there will be only one committee meeting a month (except for the month leading into our convention), I think more of our members will step up and agree to get involved. And if we vow to start and end on time and keep every meeting to less than ninety minutes, that will make volunteering even more attractive."

Why Don't We Keep It Concise?

Every word must tell.

WILLIAM STRUNK JR. AND E. B. WHITE,
AUTHORS OF *THE ELEMENTS OF STYLE*

You may be wondering, *if we agree that keeping things concise is the best way to capture and keep people's attention, why don't we do it more often?*

Good question. An Intrigue Agency project manager, Mo Sahoo, has a theory about why it's hard for us to be concise. He says, "Students are penalized for getting to the point in school. If the teacher gives you a twenty-page assignment, you better turn in twenty pages. If you turn in less, you're graded down. It doesn't matter if your ten pages are brilliant and better than everyone else's twenty. You didn't 'complete' the assignment. We're trained to become masters of 'filler' and we're rewarded for taking as long as possible to make our point."

Mo's right. We were taught to value volume. And, of course, rewarded behavior gets repeated, so many of us continue to perceive length as an indication we "did our homework."

If you want people's attention in today's culture of LFT (low frustration tolerance), it's in your best interests to reverse the belief that more is better. If you're long, you're gone. Piling on works only in rugby. Remember, no one will ever be angry at you for taking less time than expected. If they want more detail, they'll ask. From now on, shorter is better.

Action Questions: Keep It Brief or They'll Give You Grief

Does anybody really know what time it is? Does anybody really care?

LYRICIST ROBERT LAMM, CHICAGO

1. How long is that communication on your W5 Form scheduled to take? Can you ask for a brief amount of people's time and attention so they're motivated to give it to you?

2. Could you pleasantly surprise people by saying, "I can only imagine how busy you are, so I've distilled my _____ into _____ (less time than they expected?)"

3. How will you swaddle and ThunderShirt your communication to win trust because it's time-efficient? Will you put measurable boundaries on emails and meetings so they're a productive use of people's attention? Will you use five-sentence emails? Give yourself and team members three minutes to report out so meetings start and end on time?

Part IV

INTRIGUE

R = REPEATABLE

If People Can't REPEAT It, They Didn't Get It

True communication isn't what you say. It's what the receiver takes away.

CREATIVITY COACH TOM MONAHAN

It's not enough to earn people's attention in the moment.

You want to continue to earn people's attention in the moments (and months) ahead.

The goal is for people to be so intrigued with you, your idea and offering that they voluntarily choose to share it with others, thereby giving it and you a long tail of influence.

This section shows how to craft enduring communications that keep you and your message top-of-mind instead of out-of-sight, out-of-mind.

Chapter 11

Create a Phrase-that-Pays

If you see something, say something.
SAFETY CAMPAIGN FOR METROPOLITAN TRANSIT AUTHORITY

Garry Marshall, the director of the film *Pretty Woman* (which has grossed more than $463 million worldwide), said something so profound during his Maui Writers Conference keynote that I remember it as if he said it this morning. He said, "Hollywood directors can predict when their movies will make money. The question is, 'Do people walk out of the theater repeating something they heard, word for word?'"

Think about it. If you walk out of a movie voluntarily repeating its signature sound-bite, (for example, "Make my day," "I'll be back," or "Show me the money") you're taking it viral. If someone asks, "Seen any good movies lately?" you're talking about that movie in a way that motivates others to want to see it. You've become a word-of-mouth advertiser for it, all because its screenwriter crafted a catchy phrase-that-pays that stuck in your mind.

Garry Marshall's insight about the power of a memorable sound-bite applies to all interactions, whether they're on the stage, page, or online. When people watch your video, read your article, look at your website, can they repeat anything they read or you said word-for-word?

If not, what you said didn't make any lasting impression. It didn't have attention staying power. If you want your message to hold people's attention over time, craft a phrase-that-pays they voluntarily repeat and retweet.

What's a Phrase-that-Pays?

No matter what message you're about to deliver ... the goal is always to establish common ground.

FORMER US SECRETARY OF STATE MADELEINE ALBRIGHT

What's a phrase-that-pays? It's an easy-to-repeat sound-bite that resonates. The word *resonate* means "to have extended effect or impact beyond that which is apparent." That's what you want. Instead of your words going in one ear, out the other, you want a phrase that connects with people and creates common ground. A phrase-that-pays also:

- Succinctly sums up the message you want people to remember

- Distills the action you want people to take in eight words or less

- Resonates with people so they voluntarily share it with others, taking it viral

- Works as a title that can be merchandized and monetized to create a financial payoff

The right words at the right time can not only earn the attention of distracted individuals, they can change lives for the better. The moving anthem that Nikki Giovanni provided for a distraught Virginia Tech community demonstrated that.

Connect People with the Right Words at the Right Time

I find hope in the darkest days, focus in the brightest.

NOBEL PEACE PRIZE WINNER THE DALAI LAMA

On April 16, 2007, a disturbed young man roamed the campus and halls of Virginia Tech with two handguns. He ended up killing thirty-two people and injuring seventeen more, before taking his own life.

As you can imagine, this was a devastating event for VT's students, faculty, staff, and families. My sons Tom and Andrew were both on campus the day this happened. Thankfully, they were both safe. They called home the following day to tell me about the inspiring memorial service that took place on campus at Cassell Coliseum. The first few speakers spoke of the horror, the tragedy, the nightmare, spiraling everyone at the ceremony into even darker despair.

Then, VT professor Nikki Giovanni got up to speak. As a poet, Nikki understood the power of the right words at the right time to move people from feeling helplessness to feeling hopeful. With a strong, sure voice, she shared a poem she had written the night before, which included:

> We will continue to invent the future
> Through our blood and tears
> Through all this sadness
> We are the Hokies
> We will prevail
> We will prevail
> We will prevail
> We are Virginia Tech.[14]

Tom and Andrew told me, "Everyone in the crowd rose as one and started chanting along with her, "We are Virginia Tech, We will prevail." Nikki Giovanni transformed the mood of the group by reframing what happened and focusing them on the future.

Nikki Giovanni's words didn't stop there. Her rally cry was picked up by the retailers in town, who posted, "We are Virginia Tech, We will prevail" banners in their windows. Students and faculty wore wristbands with that mantra as a reminder to focus on what they could do instead of what they couldn't. Those words lifted people's spirits, connected them as a community, and moved them forward.

Five Steps to Crafting a Memorable Rally Cry

*I know that books I have written will still resonate in
50 years. I strongly feel that, as a novelist, you have a
platform and the ability to change people's minds.*

AUTHOR JODI PICOULT

Are you thinking, *I'm no Nikki Giovanni; how can I craft words that have
that kind of impact?*

You don't have to be a novelist, poet, or wordsmith to craft an
enduring rally cry that changes the way people feel and act. Every time
you communicate, you have an opportunity to introduce something
that positively influences others. I know that sounds idealistic, it's also
realistic.

In the twenty years I've had the privilege of coaching people on
how to be more concise and compelling, I've witnessed the dramatic
difference it can make when you invest the effort to create a memorable
rally cry and call to action. The following five criteria can help you craft
a phrase-that-pays that reinforces your message and resonates with
people for a long time to come.

1. Distill: Condense your call to action into eight words or less.

What do you want people to remember, feel, start, or stop? If they did
only one thing differently as a result of your message, what do you want
that to be? Condense that into a single sentence with a verb to prompt
people to take desired action. Edit it down into a tight eight words or less.

2. Rhythm: Put your words into a beat so they're easy to repeat.

Think of your phase-that-pays as a jigsaw puzzle. At first the words don't
fit, but if you talk out loud while experimenting with different combi-
nations, they will fall into place and sound *right*. Say out loud, "If you
see something, say something." Feel how easily those words roll off the

tongue? Keep playing with variations until your ears tell you you've found the perfect combination because you wouldn't change a thing.

When you make it easy and fun for people to repeat your message, they're self-motivated to bring it to the attention of others, which produces bottom-line results for you and your priority. *This Week* magazine reported the "What happens in Las Vegas, stays in Las Vegas" slogan is "one of the most quoted, talked about, and recognized ad campaigns in any industry"[15] and has generated *billions* of dollars in additional revenue. That phrase-that-pays has paid off.

3. Alliteration: Use words that start with the same sound.

Have you ever put one of those "cardboard insulating sleeves" around a hot cup of coffee so you didn't burn your fingers? Entrepreneur Jay Sorenson saw an opportunity. He knew it's hard to build a business around an unpronounceable name and that alliteration makes things memorable. So he named his product *Java Jackets* and cornered the market. In fact, he says, "Customers who meant to call our competitor call us because they can't remember our competitor's name."

Wouldn't it be nice to have people calling you because they remember your name? Wouldn't it be nice to have people taking your message viral because it's fun to repeat and retweet? Increase the chance of that happening by using words that start with the same sound.

4. Rhyme: Use rhyme if you want to be remembered over time.

The US government was concerned about the number of injuries in car accidents. So they launched a public service campaign to convince people to wear their safety belts. Its name? *Buckle Up for Safety.* Yawn. Back to the drawing board.

Second time around, they incorporated rhyme and rhythm. Are you familiar with the iconic phrase *Click It or Ticket*? That intriguing phrase not only got people's attention, but compliance went *up* and injuries went *down*,[16] proving that a well-crafted phrase-that-pays isn't just "silly semantics." It can change behavior for the better. It can even change and save lives.

5. Pause and punch: deliver your phrase-that-pays with distinctive inflection.

Be sure not to rush and blush when delivering your rally cry. People often race through high-stakes communications because they're nervous. They're subconsciously trying to get the presentation "over with." No one will register your rally cry if it gets buried in a barrage.

Arthur Levine, editor at Scholastic of J. K. Rowling (author of the *Harry Potter* series), heard me emcee an event and said, "Sam, I like the way you speak. You put *space* around your words."

When it's time to deliver your big idea, put ... space ... around your words. Pause until everyone's waiting for it ... deliver it ... then pause for three more seconds so people give it their full attention and have time to absorb it and imprint it.

Another way to make sure your phrase-that-pays stands out is to:

- ◆ Draw attention to it with "The most surprising revelation from our research was ..."

- ◆ Say, "Please write this down so you can share it with your staff...."

- ◆ Verbally highlight it with "The most important thing I've learned is ..."

- ◆ Spotlight it with "If you remember anything from my program today, I hope it's this."

If you *pause* before your phrase-that-pays, *punch* it by articulating each syllable, and then pause for three more beats, people will be able to repeat it after hearing it once.

Writing? Put your phrase-that-pays in a one-line paragraph so it pops off the page.

Please understand: coining a phrase-that-pays that has rhythm, alliteration, inflection and rhyme is not trivial. It can get what you care about remembered, shared, and acted upon.

Here's a final example of all the good things that can happen if you distill your wisdom into a repeatable legacy message that scales the attention and impact of your message.

Will Your Message Leave a Legacy?

I can't just be the girl who sang, "I Kissed a Girl."
I've got to leave a legacy.
SINGER KATY PERRY

Katy's right. We all hope to make a difference, to feel we've left a legacy that's added value in an enduring way. Neil Gaiman, the 2012 commencement speaker for Pennsylvania's University of the Arts, did that with a profoundly insightful talk and three carefully selected words.

Gaiman told the crowd that early in his career, bestselling author Stephen King got in touch to tell him "This is really great. You should enjoy it."

Neil confessed to the graduates, "'And I didn't . . . There wasn't a moment for the next fourteen years I wasn't writing something in my head, or wondering about it. And I didn't stop and look around and go, *this is really fun* . . . There were parts of the ride I missed, because I was too worried about things going wrong . . . I wish you luck . . . [B]e wise . . . Leave the world more interesting for your being here. *Make good art.*"[17]

Gaiman's admission and three words of advice to make good art was seen by more than a million people and was turned into a bestselling book entitled, *Make Good Art.* All because Gaiman crystallized his most important lessons learned into a succinct, repeatable legacy message that will outlive him.[18]

Let's put this in perspective. How many graduations have you attended? Do you remember *anything* of what was said? If you can't, it had little or no impact. People forgetting what was said may be the norm. But why be content with the norm? Why not be like Neil Gaiman and craft a meaningful message that gets remembered?

Author Leo Rosten said, "The purpose of life is to matter; to feel it's made some difference you have lived at all." If you want your message to do more than just get people's attention; if you want it to matter, then invest the time to craft a memorable phrase-that-pays that motivates people to do something differently so they reap real-world value from your work.

Action Questions: Create a Phrase-that-Pays

Memories of our works and deeds will continue in others.
CIVIL RIGHTS PIONEER ROSA PARKS

1. In looking at your W5 Form, have you already developed a meaningful phrase-that-pays that resonates so it will endure, go viral, and continue to impact others? What is that?

2. Test the memorability of your message by asking someone you trust, "What do you remember of this?" If they can't repeat something word-for-word, it means you and your message will be out-of-sight, out-of-mind. Back to the drawing board. This time, use rhythm, alliteration, inflection, and rhyme so it stays top-of-mind.

Part V

INTRIGUE

I =INTERACT

Don't Just Inform, INTERACT

No one of us is as smart as all of us.

JAPANESE PROVERB

A premise of this book is that people who grew up with the Internet are accustomed to controlling and customizing their "user experience."

They really don't want to be informed as much as they want to be involved.

They don't just want downloads of what we know; they want opportunities to interact and share what they know.

It's time to disrupt the traditional top-down, "I'm in charge, you're not" mentality.

The speaker or meeting chair is not the only expert in the room.

To the degree we create a community where everyone has an opportunity to connect, contribute to, and customize their experience, is to the degree people feel intrigued, engaged, and involved.

This section introduces a variety of ways to do that by turning one-way communications into two-way interactions.

Chapter 12

Never Again Deliver an Elevator Speech

*There are two kinds of people in this world. Those who
walk into a room and say, "Here I am" and those who
walk into a room and say, "There you are."*

ADVICE COLUMNIST ANN LANDERS

An IT executive approached me before a program and said, "I'm going to tell you something I haven't told many people. I'm an introvert. I go to conferences like this all the time, but I often bug out of the group meals and receptions because I don't have the patience for small talk."

"You're not alone. A colleague, Jennifer Kahnweiler, wrote an excellent book about that titled *The Introverted Leader.* She believes many professionals are closet introverts who are out of their element in social situations and business networking events."

He said, "Another reason I don't enjoy meeting people is I can never explain what I do in a way people get it. It's always so awkward."

I asked, "Want to brainstorm a new way to introduce yourself that isn't awkward, that can actually lead to an intriguing conversation and meaningful connection?"

He said, "Is that a rhetorical question?"

I said, "From now on, when people ask, 'What do you do?' don't tell them. That's like trying to explain electricity. Instead, you're going to ask people how they might have experienced the results of what you do. What *are* the results that people can see, smell, taste, and touch?

He thought about it and mentioned credit cards, online purchases, and computers. A light bulb went off in my mind. "Do you make the software that makes it safe for us to buy stuff online?"

He lit up. "Yes! That's exactly what I do."

"Don't tell people that. If you say, 'I make the software that makes it safe for people to buy things online,' people will go, 'Oh,' and that'll be the end of the conversation. You don't want to end the conversation. You want to jump-start the conversation."

"So what do I say?"

"Say, 'Have you, a friend, or a family member ever bought anything online, like on iTunes, Travelocity, or Amazon?' You just increased the odds they know someone who has experienced what you do. They may say, 'I never shop online. But my wife's on Amazon all the time. She loves the free shipping.'

"Confirm that connection with 'Well, our company makes the software that makes it safe for your wife to buy things on Amazon.' They not only get what you do, they relate to what you do and could even tell others what you do. All in sixty seconds and in a dialogue, not a monologue."

He actually got a little misty-eyed, and said, "I can't wait to get home after this event."

"Why?"

"I finally have a way to tell my eight-year-old son what I do so he can understand it."

Realize What People Want when They Ask "What Do You Do?"

It's no longer about you. It wasn't to begin with.
ACTRESS DIANE KEATON

His story about what it meant to him to be able to connect with his son is a reminder this issue is not petty, it's profound. Whether we like it or not, wherever we go, the people we meet will ask "What do you do?" What we need to understand is, they're not really trying to find out about our work; they're trying to find out what we have in common, so they have a hook on which to hang a mutually interesting conversation.

This is why, from now on, you must never again give an elevator speech. Do you know anyone who likes listening to a *speech*? An elevator speech is a monologue delivered in the presence of witnesses. An elevator conversation is a dialogue that leads to a meaningful connection.

This was a real epiphany for a participant in my *POP! Your Communication* workshop at the INC 500/5000 conference. We were brainstorming elevator conversations, and I asked Colleen, Entrepreneur of the Year for her state, "What do you do?"

Two minutes later, none of us had any idea what she did, and she was the CEO. Think of the millions of dollars of lost opportunity costs. She was surrounded by successful entrepreneurs, but none of us would remember her, refer her, or walk up to her afterward to explore a partnership.

I asked, "What are the *real-world results* of what you do that we can see, smell, taste, or touch? "

She said, "I run medical facilities that offer MRIs and CT scans."

"That's good because it's real world; we can *see* what you're talking about. But don't stop there because we haven't yet created a personal connection. Turn that description into a three-part question: 'Have you, a friend, or a family member ever had an MRI or a CT scan?'"

"What's this about a three-part question?"

"If you ask, 'Have *you* ever had an MRI or CT scan?' and they haven't, you just ran into a conversation cul de sac. Three-part questions increase the likelihood the person will know someone who is familiar with, or has benefitted from, what you or your organization does.

Imagine the other person says, "Yeah, my daughter hurt her knee playing soccer. She had an MRI." This links what you do to what the person just said. "Oh, I run the medical facilities that offer MRIs, like the one your daughter had when she hurt her knee playing soccer."

"Ahh," they'll probably say. Believe me, an intrigued "ahh" is a lot better than a confused "huh?" or an apathetic "ohh." They relate to what you do, are more likely to remember you, and if they ever need an MRI or CT scan, they're more likely to contact you because people like to do business with people they know and like.

How Are You Relating to People?

People respond in accordance with how you relate to them.
ACTIVIST NELSON MANDELA

A quick-witted twenty-something demonstrated how quickly you can make a connection if you ask a question instead of trying to explain something that's complicated.

I was on a speaking tour with my sons, who were teenagers at the time. We had a night free in Denver, so went downstairs to the hotel lobby to ask the concierge, "What do you suggest?"

He took one look at Tom and Andrew and said, "You've got to go to D & B's."

We were from Maui at the time and had never heard of D & B's. We said, "What's that?"

He must have instinctively known that trying to explain it would have been a lost cause. If he'd said, "Well, it's kind of like a sports bar, but it's also an indoor amusement park with a restaurant and pool tables and video games and bowling lanes," he would have lost us at hello.

Instead, he asked a qualifying question, "Have you ever been to Chuck E. Cheese?"

My sons nodded enthusiastically, "It's one of our favorite places."

He smiled and said, "D & B's *is like a Chuck E. Cheese for adults.*"

Bingo. Ten seconds and we knew exactly what it was and wanted to go there. They should have put him on commission.

What do you and your co-workers say when asked, "What do you do?" Do your responses elicit furrowed eyebrows? If so, you're losing opportunities to create mutually rewarding relationships for yourself and your organization. Turn your next staff meeting into a brainstorming session where everyone has opportunities to develop a variety of ways to introduce themselves so people relate to what you do and want to continue the conversation.

Action Questions: Never Again Deliver an Elevator Speech

It's all about paying attention. Attention is vitality.
It connects you with others. It makes you eager.
Stay eager.
AUTHOR SUSAN SONTAG

1. How will you replace a one-way elevator speech with two-way elevator intros that turn a monologue into a dialogue? How can you put the results of what you do in a three-part question to give people a chance to share how they, or someone they know, might have experienced or benefitted from what you do?

2. How can you remind yourself to listen to what people say and then link what you do to what they just said so you confirm the connection and create an intriguing conversation?

Chapter 13

Create Mutually Rewarding Conversations

*You can make more friends in two months by becoming
interested in other people than you can in two years
by trying to get people interested in you.*

AUTHOR DALE CARNEGIE

A client called to tell me she would be attending a high-powered meeting of CEOs at the Tower Club in Tysons Corner and wanted to know if I could help her prepare. Could I?!

Maria is a financial adviser who presents money management workshops for corporations. She told me, "Sam, I'm not going to know anyone there. Frankly, I'm a little intimidated by this group, and I want to make the most of it instead of ending up being a wallflower in a corner."

I said, "Done. Get a copy of the January–February 2012 *Harvard Business Review* issue, which contains 'The Economics of Well-Being.' It's got articles with metrics that show the bottom-line benefits of 'soft skills.'[19] They cite research showing that the happier people are with their finances and health, the higher their morale, performance, and productivity."

"Are you suggesting I take that magazine with me to the Tower Club?"

"Have it in your purse but don't take it out unless it's appropriate. When you walk in, look around for a small group of people you'd like to join, people who seem to be enjoying one another's company but aren't in a private conversation. Walk over and stand an arm's length away."

"Why an arm's length away?"

"Because you don't want to get into 'their space' without asking first. If you stand there with a pleasant expression on your face, the person speaking or the person closest to you will look at you, which is your opportunity to say, 'Okay if I listen in?'

"This is a diplomatic way of letting them know you're not crashing their party; you're asking permission. In all my years of doing this, no one has ever said, 'No!'

"Then, wait your turn until you can add value to what was just said. If someone brings up job performance, you can say, 'Did any of you see the January-February double issue of *Harvard Business Review*?'

"Someone might say, 'I got a copy for all my managers,' at which you can say, 'Wasn't it a great issue? What did you find most interesting about it?' If no one's seen the issue, introduce a particularly intriguing quote or finding that relates to what was just being discussed."

Maria said, "Okay, I'll try it."

The following week I got a phone call from an excited Maria. "Sam, they fought over me! I did just what you said. When it was time for dinner, one of them asked if I would sit with him at his table. Another person in the group said, 'Hey, I was the one who said she could listen in!'"

Don't you love it when a plan works?

Don't Be Intimidated, Be Intrigued

Maybe everybody in the whole damn world is scared of each other.
AUTHOR JOHN STEINBECK

An engineer told me, "When I was a kid, I couldn't wait to grow up because I thought confidence came with the territory. I thought, once I got to be an adult, I would never again feel self-conscious or worry what to talk about. Boy, was I wrong. Where can I get a confidence pill?"

I told him, "The way to get a confidence pill is to approach conversations like a caring journalist. Journalists aren't scared to meet anyone because they know how to sidestep chit-chat and genuinely engage people. They ask 'W' questions, listen intently to what's being said, and follow up with related questions that get to the heart of the matter."

He said, "Sounds great, but how can I do that?"

Here are the four suggestions I gave him on how to get past platitudes (which no one finds intriguing) and create meaningful conversations and connections.

1. No more standard openers.

Bland questions get bland answers. Try, "What are you working on that you're excited about?" or "What do you do on weekends?"

2. Ask for advice.

Magazine founder Malcolm Forbes said, "The way to a man's heart is through his opinion." The way to anyone's heart is through their advice. Asking "What do you suggest?" sends the message you think this person has wisdom to share and you welcome it. Instead of swapping platitudes, you're on your way to a productive exchange.

3. Use the two magic words, "Tell me."

Many people start conversations with closed questions that relegate the other person to giving one-word responses.

"Did you enjoy the Chamber of Commerce meeting?" "Yeah."

The two words, "Tell me" transform a "skim the surface" exchange into a deeper, more meaningful conversation where you really get to know a person.

"I missed that Chamber of Commerce meeting. Could you tell me about it?"

4. Turn back more conversations than you take back.

Every time someone finishes talking, you have a choice. You either *take* back the conversation with an "I" statement or *turn* back the conversation with a "You" question. If you consistently *take* back conversations, you take the wind out of the other person's conversational sails.

For example, "Who's the president of the Chamber these days?"

"Judy Gray."

"Oh, I know Judy. She lives in our neighborhood. I'll always remember the time..."

Sigh. "I" statements keep the attention focused on what we feel, think, know, or have done.

Feel the difference when you *turn* back the conversation with a "You" question.

"Oh, Judy is the president. What are her goals for the Chamber this year?"

"You" questions keep attention focused on *the other person*. People will feel you're genuinely interested in getting to know them because you *are*.

Create Intriguing Conversations that Bring Out the Best in Yourself and Others

My best friend is the one who brings out the best in me.

ENTREPRENEUR HENRY FORD

A gruff workshop participant told me, "I don't like these techniques. They feel contrived to me."

I told him, "I'm glad you brought this up because it gives me an opportunity to clarify these techniques are *not* meant to be formulaic or manipulative. They are not tactics. They are tools grounded in a sincere intent to bypass superficial chit-chat and genuinely connect with people. It would be wonderful if meeting people came naturally, yet many of us still find it awkward.

"These approaches can help you acquire the *skill* of creating genuinely intriguing conversations. Because it is a *skill,* just like playing the piano. When you learn to play the piano, you often start by learning scales. After practicing the scales, you get to the point where your fingers know the keys so well that you don't even have to think about where to put them; you just make beautiful music.

"The same is true with learning to make conversational music. Once you learn the keys of 'Tell me' and 'Turn back' versus 'Take back,' you won't even think about them anymore; they'll be part of who you are and how you show up."

A recent college grad is testimony to the power of using these ideas to turn strangers into friends. Mo told me, "I didn't enjoy my first six months in Washington D.C. I thought it was such an unfriendly place. I'd go to bars to meet people, which made no sense because I don't drink, and you can't hear what anyone says over the noise, anyway.

"Then you told me, 'Everyone is waiting for someone else to make the first move.' I decided to become the 'convener' and initiate activities I wanted to be part of. I asked people what they wanted to do on weekends, and then I organized it. Now, we have a huge circle of friends who go rafting, play fantasy football, and have game nights. None of us feel lonely anymore because we always have something interesting going on."

If You Can't Converse, You Can't Connect

Small talk is far from being small or trivial. It is the salve of a disconnected society, a cornerstone of civility.
BERNADO J. CARDUCCI, DIRECTOR OF SHYNESS INSTITUTE AT
INDIANA UNIVERSITY SOUTHEAST

Let's put this topic in perspective. In an excellent article in *Science Daily,* shyness expert Bernado Carducci posited that many of us dislike meeting people because we have unrealistic expectations. We think we have to be witty or brilliant, when all that is really necessary is to be "willing."[20]

That's what Mo did. He understood that "good things come to those who initiate." He realized the quality of our life is determined by the quality of our connections, and the quality of our connections depends on our willingness to create or convene quality interactions. It's on us.

Are you waiting for other people to be friendly? As Dr. Phil would say, "How's that working for you?" Why not choose to be the one who creates and convenes intriguing interactions? If you are willing to invest the time and effort to get good at this; you will be able to go anywhere, anytime, and meet anyone with peace of mind because you'll be confident in your ability to create mutually rewarding conversations and connections that are a win for all involved.

Action Questions: Create Mutually Rewarding Conversations

If we have no peace, it is because we have forgotten we belong to each other.

MOTHER TERESA

1. Do you enjoy meeting people? What do you do to create meaningful conversations and connections? How do you show that you're genuinely intrigued in others?

2. What is a public event you've got coming up where you'll be meeting people? How will you remember to turn back versus take back conversations to draw people out and create more meaningful connections instead of staying on the surface with small talk?

3. How will you become a convener? How will you stop waiting for other people to make the first move and be the one who initiates the activities everyone wants to be part of?

Chapter 14

Facilitate Interactive Meetings and Programs

I've had a wonderful evening, but this wasn't it.

COMEDIAN GROUCHO MARX

Did you see the 2014 Academy Awards? Host Ellen DeGeneres delighted 43 million viewers by turning a three-hour marathon of "thank-you" speeches into a delightfully interactive evening that *was* wonderful. She ordered pizza (really!) and had it delivered to the theater, where she handed out paper plates and napkins (with the help of Brad Pitt) to some of the planet's biggest movie stars including Meryl Streep, George Clooney, and Julia Roberts.

She asked people in the audience ("Come on, Harvey Weinstein, get out your wallet. I *know* you've got money") for some cash to pay for it and took a selfie (now being called a *groufie*) with Kevin Spacey, Jared Leto, and others that was retweeted millions of times in the next hour.[21]

Instead of running the show, Ellen gave the audience a chance to *be* the show. Good for Ellen for realizing it's passé to force people to be passive. She created an experience where people were on the edge of their seats due to the sheer unpredictability of what was happening. Ellen's interactive approach not only paid off in improved ratings (as heralded in a Yahoo! headline the next day, "Oscar viewership the best since 2000"[22]), but it made a statement, answering the following questions: Why run programs the way they've always been run? Why not showcase attendees as much as the emcee? Why not involve people instead of simply informing them?

Give People Opportunities to Control and Contribute

I get a little itchy if I don't have some control.

ACTRESS AMY POEHLER

These days, *everyone* gets itchy if they don't have some control. That's why it is smart to share control instead of always taking control of your meetings and events. Notice, I'm not saying *lose or give away* control; I'm saying *share* control. Here's how.

When I lived in Hawaii, I had an opportunity to work with visionary leader Mike White and his team at the Ka'anapali Beach Hotel. KBH did not have the glitziest property on Maui, but it did have an incredibly high percentage of returning guests. Why?

Visitors felt they were experiencing the real "aloha" of the islands. Employees gathered in the lobby every day at noon to sing, dance hula, and play the ukulele. Guests were greeted by name and treated to fresh papayas, bananas, guava, and protea from the staff's yards.

As general manager, Mike felt it was important for employees to be *ohana* (Hawaiian for "family") so he held monthly all-hands meetings to keep everyone updated. This was a logistical challenge because it meant paying employees to come in on their day off and temporarily having a "bare bones" operation while staffers participated. In spite of this, Mike put KBH's money and schedule where its values were and committed to doing this.

Instead of running all the meetings himself (the default approach of most bosses), he divvied up the leadership among the different department heads. One month the marketing director was in charge, the next month the food and beverage manager, the next the head of housekeeping, and so forth.

The hosts had complete autonomy. Let the creativity begin! It became a mini-contest to see who could facilitate the most intriguing meeting. Everyone looked forward to attending because they never knew what to expect. It also developed the staff members' speaking and leadership skills.

How about you? Do you always chair your staff meetings? Would it create a more engaged workplace if you rotated hosts and gave employees an opportunity to take the lead?

This is not petty. An August 31, 2014, CBS *Sunday Morning* feature interviewed Robert Levering, cocreator of the *Fortune 100 Best Places to Work* about whether there's a connection between workers being well treated and the bottom line. The answer was an emphatic yes.

Levering cited a Gallup poll that found only "three out of ten employees are actively engaged, meaning they're committed to or enthusiastic about their work," and quoted another study that found "disengaged workers are costing US companies $550 billion."[23]

Are you engaging employees and giving them opportunities to be part of the planning instead of apart *from* the planning, or are you simply telling them what's new and what to do?

Are You Taking Control or Sharing Control of Your Meetings?

When I was a kid, there was no collaboration; it's you with a camera bossing your friends around. But as an adult, filmmaking is all about appreciating the talents of the people around you and knowing you could never have made these films by yourself.

DIRECTOR STEVEN SPIELBERG

A colleague gave some push-back to this idea of sharing control. He said, "We're always in a time crunch, so our goal is to get in and get out. I'm the only one who knows everything that's going on. Plus, I'm the boss. I'm supposed to run the meetings."

I told him, "I understand that's the way it's always been done, but things have changed." Most people today grew up on the Internet, which is a democracy. Everyone has a voice. Everyone creates and customizes their "user" experience and pays attention only to what appeals to them. People today are accustomed to being in control. They post what they want, when they want it—on YouTube, Facebook, Twitter, Pinterest. They create their own music stations on Pandora. They don't passively watch their favorite TV programs like *American Idol* or *Dancing with the Stars*; they determine the fate of contestants by voting who stays and who goes. They cocreate the show.

Then they sit in a meeting and have *no* control, *no* opportunity to cocreate things. As a result, they tune out, even if they're still sitting there.

In fact, an August 18, 2014, *Harvard Business Review* article by Gretchen Gavett entitled "What People are Really Doing when They're on a Conference Call" revealed some intriguing (and distressing?) statistics including, "27% of people admitted to falling asleep during conference calls, and 13% 'outed' themselves by confessing they were actually at a race track, a wedding rehearsal, a truck stop bathroom, grilling and getting a tan, in a fitting room trying on clothes (and my personal favorite), 'chasing my dog down the street because she got out of the house.'"[24]

This would be funny if this inattention and lack of engaged participation didn't represent millions in lost productivity for these workers' organizations.

What to do? The article quotes author Keith Ferrazzi's suggestion to organizers to "implement a 'Take 5' at the beginning of meetings and conference calls and dedicate five minutes to giving everyone an opportunity to take turns and talk a little about what's going on their lives, either personally or professionally. This gets people in the mood to actually listen to each other."

Connecting Is Not a Spectator Sport

Whoever does the most talking has the most fun.

RUTH REED (SAM HORN'S MOM)

From now on, any time you conduct a gathering, ask yourself, "Instead of doing all the talking, how can I make this a two-way interaction instead of a one-way download of information?"

That's what Miki Agrawal did to transform her book-signing into a fun, interactive experience. Instead of reading from her book (boring,) she asked the audience if they'd like to play *Inside the Author's Studio*. Everyone got to be James Lipton (the host of the Bravo series *Inside the Actors Studio*). Instead of being spectators, they became interviewers and asked, "Did you ever have a dark night of the soul?" "How did you get your agent?" "How can we get the book in us out of us?" Everyone was engaged from start to finish because *they* were doing most of the talking.

A woman at Miki's book launch put her hand up and said, "I'm sitting here in awe at what's happening in this room. This would never happen where I'm from. If I told someone I was writing a book, they'd say, 'Who are you to write a book? You're no F. Scott Fitzgerald.' It is so encouraging to see how everyone is truly celebrating you instead of being jealous of you."

She brought up such a good point. Actress Bette Midler was asked, "What's the hardest part of success?" She said, "Finding someone who's genuinely happy for you."

When we watch someone be the "star," it can be tempting to feel jealous because we have no part in that person's success. He or she is the expert; we're not. But when the person in charge chooses to level the playing field and give everyone a chance to participate, we're *part* of his or her success.

Set a Precedent for
Meaningful Participation

Community makes the world run.

MUSICIAN QUESTLOVE

Are you a meeting planner, emcee, or speaker? Do you create a community where audience members get to contribute, customize their experience, and connect? Do you set up a *scenius*? That's a half-and-half word musician Brian Eno coined that means "half-scene, half-genius."

As the host, you can access and elevate the "genius" in the room by giving people opportunities to feed off one another's experience, expertise, and energy.

All too often, though, that doesn't happen. In fact, the research of Columbia psychologists Paul Ingram and Michael Morris reveals that, even though executives said their purpose for attending a networking event was to "meet as many different people as possible," they actually tended to talk to "the few other guests they knew well" instead of making new connections.[25]

Think about that. Companies spend big money every year to fly employees to conventions, trade shows, and training programs and pay for hotels, meals, and registration fees. Yet once there, they tend to sit next to and hang out with people they already know. This defeats a primary purpose of attending a public event, which is to expand your network and form *new* relationships.

It gets worse. *Inc. Magazine* staff writer Jill Krasney found many people feel networking at business events is cringe-worthy, "sleazy," and likened it to feeling like a "used car salesman." She cites a paper in the journal *Administrative Science Quarterly* that "the idea of forming relationships to get ahead feels, well, pretty immoral. Isn't that the definition of using someone?"[26]

This is an important distinction. INTRIGUE is not about using people; it's about adding value to people. It's not about wanting something *from* people; it's wanting something *for* them. The goal isn't to get ahead; it's to get a "rising tide raising all boats" interaction that elevates all involved.

Does that sound grandiose? It doesn't have to be. Let me share my first experience of a scenius, and then I'll share a couple of suggestions on how to set up a scenius at your next business event.

Turn Business Events into a "Raising All Ships" Scenius

More business decisions occur over lunch and dinner than at any other time, yet no MBA courses are given on the subject.
BUSINESS AUTHOR PETER DRUCKER

I walked into New York City's Four Seasons Restaurant, head on a swivel, full of anticipation. Martin Edelston, founder of *Boardroom Reports* and *Bottom-Line/Personal*, had invited me to one of his famous salons, along with twenty others who had been featured in his publications.

We took our places at a long rectangular dinner table with Marty at the head. He rang the ceremonial bell next to his plate, warmly welcomed us, and explained the format. Instead of staring at our salads or talking about the weather, he proposed we each report out the most interesting trend in our industry ... in two minutes.

Thus ensued two of the most interesting hours of my life. A cardiac surgeon shared the newest advances in open heart surgery. A psychologist reported a dramatic increase in overseas adoptions and the reasons behind that. An author shared ethical ways to influence. After each person's report, Marty would follow up with a few provocative questions to add even more breadth and depth to what had been shared. He was the quintessential scenius host and facilitator.

If you're tired of going to or hosting business events where no one connects, do as Gandhi suggested and "Be the change you wish to see." Here are two changes that are sure to turn boring business events into a "raising all ships" scenius, and you don't have to be the official host like Martin Edelston, and you don't have to meet at the Four Seasons (although that would be nice).

Two Ways to Set Up a Scenius

Communication leads to community, that is, mutual valuing.
PSYCHOLOGIST ROLLO MAY

1. Start your meeting with introductions.

No "touching fingers" ice-breakers that cause people to head for the hills. Simply state, "We want this to be the friendliest, most productive program you've ever attended, so we're putting our schedule where our values are. We have an incredible brain trust in the room, and we want to give you an opportunity to tap into it by connecting with a couple of people you don't know. When I say, 'GO!' please stand up, look for two people in your area you haven't yet met, and exchange this info: 1) your name, 2) something you're looking forward to at this event, and 3) a project you're working on you're excited about. Ready, GO!"

I do this every time I emcee an event because it transforms a ballroom of anxious strangers into a ballroom of animated friends. A woman came up to me and said, "You nailed it. I was sitting there, thinking, *I flew all the way here and don't know a soul. Is this going to be a waste of time?* I connected with two other HR directors and we made plans to meet for lunch. I already feel in my gut I made the right decision to come here. And that was in the first five minutes!"

2. Create a "Table Topic Meal."

Announce *before* people take their places that this is a "sit by someone new" meal. Place cards with relevant questions at each seat and invite participants to discuss suggested topics with their neighbor(s) such as:

- What is a tangible take-away you've received from our event? How do you plan to apply it?

- What is an achievement you or your organization are particularly pleased with this year?

- What is a favorite resource you'd like to recommend that's improved your effectiveness?

Conference coordinator Ruth Stergiou takes this idea one step further and wraps up her Invent the Future Conferences with "meet the expert" round tables. Ruth says, "This is an excellent way to keep everyone engaged late in the afternoon. They get to pick two topics (for example, office politics, salary negotiation, personal branding) and two experts (for example, an Apple executive, association president, social media expert) they want to meet.

"The experts are instructed to use only five minutes of their twenty-five minutes to share a best practice, and then they facilitate a brainstorming session where everyone gets to ask for input on a priority of their choice. It is gratifying to see how animated everyone is at the end of full day."

Action Questions: Facilitate Interactive Meetings and Programs

If you had to identify, in one word, the reason why the human race has not achieved, and never will achieve, its full potential, that word would be "meetings."

HUMORIST DAVE BARRY

1. Do you chair meetings? Do you rotate the leadership and give attendees an opportunity to run the show? If so, good for you. If not, how can you make people part of the decision-making process, so, contrary to what Dave says, your meetings are participative and productive?

2. Are you tired of business events where no one really connects? Are you a meeting planner, speaker, or emcee? How will you set up a scenius so everyone gets to receive input on something meaningful to them? How will you create an interactive community and involve your audience so they have opportunities to customize their experience and contribute to one another?

Part VI

INTRIGUE

G = Give

GIVE Attention First

*When I get on stage, my first goal is not to show
my expertise; it's to give a bit of joy.*
ITALIAN TENOR ANDREA BOCELLI

Previous sections have focused on how we can *earn* quality attention from others.

This section focuses on how we can, first, *give* quality attention to others. Instead of our goal being to show our expertise; it's wiser to give others opportunities to showcase *theirs*.

This section also explores how we can find out what truly matters to the people we want to connect with so we can focus on their interests *first*.

Doing so is one of the keys to creating mutually intriguing interactions.

Chapter 15

Customize to Connect

*The blank page. The blinking cursor. Writer's block.
Sting faced it for eight years after a lifetime of fertile song-
writing. The ideas stopped. No new songs came.*

REPORTER JOHN LOGAN

Imagine not having any ideas for eight years when your livelihood depends on it. Ouch.

That's what happened to musician Sting, who Logan described in a *Vanity Fair* article as being "burned out." What did he do to break through that block? He returned to his English hometown near the shipyards of Newcastle where he grew up watching "great iron ships grow until they blotted out the sun." He let the "shipwrights, welders, and riveters speak to him and through him." As a result, Sting's creativity came alive again. He was inspired to write a new musical based on the stories he heard that opened on Broadway in 2014.[27]

Sting's experience offers a lesson for anyone who's running low on intrigue. Chances are you're not suffering from a creativity block; you're suffering from a connection block. Perhaps you, too, need to get out of your head and into the field to connect with the people you want to connect with. Perhaps it's time to stop trying to "think up stuff" and ask the individuals you want to reach what they think, what they suggest. When you do, the fount of intrigue will once again begin to flow because you're focusing on its true source, empathy not intellect.

INTRIGUE Is a Byproduct of Empathy

You can't think yourself out of a writing block; you've got to write yourself out of a thinking block.

TV/FILM WRITER JOHN ROGERS

Sometimes it doesn't work to try to write yourself out of a thinking block. That was my epiphany while rushing to meet a deadline for my *Tongue Fu!* at School book. I usually love to write. But I was busy raising two sons with a full calendar of speaking and consulting, and the words weren't coming. Writing had become hard work. I would reread what I'd written (I know, a fatal error) and think *Yuck*. I didn't like what I was producing. It didn't sing. It wasn't alive.

A blessing came in the form of an article about a TV director. For a while this director could do no wrong. He was the first to receive an Emmy for Best Comedy and Best Drama in the same year. But now his shows were sinking in the ratings as they were featuring increasingly bizarre plots his viewers couldn't relate to. The reporter posited the director had lost his golden touch because he'd lost the common touch. He had become so busy writing and directing that he'd become disconnected.

The light bulb went off in my mind. No wonder I had INTRIGUE block. Writing isn't supposed to be an isolated *intellectual* exercise; it's supposed to be an *empathetic* exercise. I was focusing on what *I* wanted to say, instead of connecting with my readers and finding out what they wanted to say. I got up, drove to my sons' high school, and crowdsourced my content.

I asked students, "What do you do if someone is teasing you or bullying you?" I asked teachers, "What do you do if a parent accuses you of not caring for his or her kid?" I asked the principal, "What's it like when a teacher or counselor says, 'I quit. I don't get paid enough to deal with this'?"

Like Sting, I let the people I wanted to connect with talk *to* and *through* me. I listened to their worries, their wishes. And when I got home, the ideas flowed out of my head so fast my fingers could hardly keep up. It was a lesson I've never forgotten.

How about you? Are you having a hard time creating content for an upcoming communication? Have your ideas dried up? Are you grinding it out because you have a deadline to meet? If your intent is simply to finish your project, you can accomplish that, but that won't make it sing. You may end up with a completed project that's lifeless, dry, disconnected.

If your goal is to connect, get up out of your chair and into the field. Reach out to those you want to connect with. Find out what keeps them up at night, and then get back to work with their voices filling your mind, flowing out onto the page.

Be sure to also ask your intended audience for their successes and best practices. Too many of the premeeting questionnaires I see focus exclusively on "What challenges/problems are you facing?" There's an implied top-down, "I'm the expert. Tell me how I can fix you" mentality to inquiring solely about what's wrong in people's life.

Ask an equal number of questions that give people an opportunity to share their insights and advice. Give them an opportunity to be the expert and contribute to the process instead of simply being passive recipients of your process.

Lead with Their Needs, Not Yours

If you're trying to persuade people to do something, it seems to me you should use the language they use every day. Write in their vernacular.
ADVERTISING GENIUS DAVID OGILVY

Another way to capture the favorable attention of decision-makers is to study their website and marketing material and use their exact language in your outreach to them.

Elon Musk, the visionary founder of Space X, gave some excellent advice about this. As soon as I saw he was scheduled to give a luncheon presentation at the National Press Club, I put it on my calendar and planned to be at one of the front tables to absorb his wisdom. I called my son Tom (the one who works for NASA) and asked, "Anything you'd like me to ask Elon Musk?"

Tom said, "Yeah. A lot of my friends who worked on the shuttle have been laid off. Many are applying to Space X." He said, only half-kidding, "Ask him the best way to get hired at Space X."

Sure enough, I had a chance to ask Tom's question in the Q & A. Musk's eloquent one-sentence answer? "Don't tell me about the positions you've held; tell me about the problems you've solved."

Musk just gave anyone paying attention the "answers to his test." If job applicants were smart, they did not send in the same-old, same-old résumés they submitted everywhere else. They customized their bullet points to highlight the specific problems they'd solved instead of the positions they'd held. Doing so would dramatically increase their odds of catching the attention of Space X decision-makers because their résumés emphasized their founder's hiring criteria.

Have Your Decision-Makers Given You the Answers to Their Test?

In school, you're taught a lesson and then given a test. In life, you're given a test that teaches you a lesson.

AUTHOR TOM BODETT

Are you applying for a job or competing for a contract? Have you studied their job description, researched their contract requirements? Have you customized your application by using *their exact words* in your application? It's amazing to me how few people do this.

This was the crux of a conversation I had with a family friend who asked me to review his Peace Corps application. Casey said, "I don't know if I have a chance, but I want to give it a try."

I said, "Okay Casey, we're going to make you as intriguing as possible to Peace Corps personnel. Bring up their website."

"Why?"

"Because they're giving you the answers to their test. See here? They bullet the characteristics and qualifications they're looking for. You're going to address every single one of those criteria and give an example of how you've done it, using *their* words. It shows them you pay attention and can be trusted to read directions and deliver what was requested."

Guess who got accepted to the Peace Corps? Guess who ended up working with school children in Guatemala, teaching them lacrosse, and loving every minute of this opportunity to make a difference? All because Casey got his employers' attention by giving them what they asked for.

Dr. Benjamin Spock was asked how he got the material for his book, *Dr. Spock's Baby and Child Care,* which Wikipedia claims has sold more than 50 million copies and was "the best-selling book in the 20th century, other than the Bible." Spock said, "I really learned it all from mothers." Dr. Spock didn't *create* his content from scratch; he crowd-sourced it by asking his intended customers what they most wanted to know, and then delivered it to them.

How about you? Ae you customizing your communication so it resonates with people? If so, you have just increased the likelihood your content will resonate with them because it came from them.

Action Questions: Customize to Connect

*If you are an artist, you try to keep an ear to
the ground and an ear to your heart.*

MUSICIAN BRUCE SPRINGSTEEN

1. Time to look at your WS Form. Who is your intended audience? How are you going to get out of *your* head and into theirs to find out what's important to them so you can customize your content?

2. How can you connect with your intended audience and let them speak to you and through you? How will you "keep your ear to the ground" your customers walk on so you can use *their* language, meet *their* needs?

Chapter 16

Listen Like You Like to Be Listened To

I don't mean to interrupt. I just remember random things and get excited.

POPULAR T-SHIRT

Years ago my sons and I were planning a holiday weekend. Should we have friends over for a backyard barbeque? Go to Lake Fairfax for the fireworks?

Tom seemed a bit distracted so I asked, "Tom, are you listening?"

"Sure, Mom," he said, "You have my *undevoted* attention."

Out of the mouths of teens. In our distracted world ("Look, there's a kitty"), the norm is to give our *undevoted* attention. This is not petty. Undevoted attention loses customers and employees. In fact, a US Department of Labor Statistics study found that 46 percent of people who quit their job said it was because they didn't feel listened to, and therefore felt unappreciated.[28]

Are You Giving Undivided or Undevoted Attention?

When people talk, listen completely. Most people never listen.

NOVELIST ERNEST HEMINGWAY

Listening completely is not only the core of charisma; it is at the heart of connection. Yet listening completely is rare. The norm is for people to interrupt, finish others' sentences, give their undevoted attention. Think about it. Of all the people you know:

- Who is someone who *really* listens to you?

- What does that person do that makes him or her such a good listener?

- How does this person make you feel when she gives you her undivided attention?

- How do you feel about that person?

Guess what? In the twenty years I've asked those questions in my workshops, most people can only think of *one or two* individuals, out of everyone they know, who really listens to them. It's that rare. Reflect for a moment on how you feel about that person who gives you her *undivided* attention. Don't you feel deeply connected to her? If you'd like to connect more deeply with the people in your life, on and off the job, these LISTEN steps can help make that happen.

The L of Listen = Look, Lift, and Lean

You can't truly listen to anyone and do anything else at the same time.

AUTHOR M. SCOTT PECK

Put down your smartphone. Turn your chair away from your computer. These actions are a way of saying to yourself and the person in front of you, "This can wait. *You* are my number-one priority."

Look fully at the person and **lift** your eyebrows. Feel how that animates your face? **Lean** forward so you're, literally and figuratively, on the edge of your seat. This indicates you're eager to hear what the person has to say. You're reaching out to him, which moves you from lethargy to curiosity. **Looking, leaning, and lifting** not only make you *look* intrigued, but these actions help you *feel* more intrigued.

The I of Listen = Ignore Everything Else

Tell yourself, "This person is my number-one priority right now. Everything else can wait." Resist the temptation to look over the person's shoulder to see who's walking by. If your eyes wander, your mind will, too.

The S of Listen = Suspend Judgment

A supervisor told me, "I've managed many of my employees for years. Whether it's fair or not, I've labeled each of them. This one is the complainer; this one is the trouble-maker. You get the idea. I already know what they're going to say when they walk into my office."

Actually, you don't know what they're going to say until *after* they've said it. Think to yourself, *Give her a chance* or *Hear her out* to help you pay attention to what the person is saying *this* time instead of thinking about what he or she said *last* time. You might want to follow the example of ad man Bill Bernbach. If he found himself disagreeing with someone, he would pull out a piece of paper he kept in his jacket pocket and peek at it. It said these four words, "They might be right."[29]

The T of Listen = Take Notes

Our twenty-something neighbor was interviewing for a graduate program at Georgetown University. Cat told me, "I've got so much riding on this meeting. How can I make a good impression?"

"Take a quality notebook in and take notes when they emphasize their priorities. For example, if the interviewer says, 'We've got hundreds of applications, why should we pick you?' refer to your notes and say, 'You mentioned earlier you like your grad students to have leadership experience. Well, I have worked for Reston Tennis Association the past two years, and…'"

The happy ending to that story? Cat is now a happy grad student at GU. She told me, "There was a bonus to taking notes. Instead of feeling self-conscious and wondering, *Where should I look? What should I do with my hands?* it gave me something to do so I didn't get nervous."

The E of Listen = Empathize

Finding it hard to pay attention? Ask yourself these four words, "*How would I feel?*"

"*How would I feel* if this were happening to me? *How would I feel* if I were in this person's shoes? We may not agree with or like how someone's behaving; those four words help us understand it.

The N of Listen = No Buts about It

How do you feel when someone tells you: "I hear what you're saying, but …." "I know this is important to you, but …." "I'm sorry this happened, but…." "You did a good job on that, but…."

The word *but* cancels out whatever was said before it. Doesn't it? That little word does more damage than almost any word in the English language because it dismisses what the other person is saying. Consider banishing that word from your vocabulary. People will never feel you're really paying attention as long as your response has a *but* in it.

Replace *but* with the word *and*. For example, "I hear what you're saying, and…." "I know how important this is to you, and…." "I'm sorry this happened, and…." See and feel the difference? The word *but* argues. The word *and* acknowledges.

The Enduring Benefits of Intrigued Listening

*For most people, the opposite of talking is not
listening; it's waiting for their turn to talk.*

AUTHOR FRAN LEBOWITZ

And now, I get to tell two stories that show how giving someone our intrigued attention can create a mutually rewarding connection. A workshop participant wrote me after our program and said, "Those four words, 'How would I feel?' changed my relationship with my mother. She has been in a rest home for the last several years. I used to dread driving out to see her every Saturday because all she ever did was complain. Complained about her roommate, about her aches and pains, that no one ever came to see her. I had pretty much stopped listening to her.

"When you shared those four words in your program, I asked myself, '*How would I feel* if I were in bed eighteen hours a day, seven days a week? *How would I feel* if I lived six feet away from someone I didn't like, who played the TV so loud I couldn't hear myself think? *How would I feel* if every morning I woke up, I hurt, and I couldn't see a day when that wasn't going to be the case?'

"It moved me right out of my impatience. When I took the time to consider what my mom's days were like and all she's done for me, I realized it's the least I can do to spend a couple hours with her every week and be more supportive."

There's more to that story. He said, "You said that part of being a better listener is to be proactive and create what we would like instead of reactively complaining about what we don't like. I asked myself, 'What *would* I like?' What I wanted was to talk about good times. So that next Saturday, I took a photo album with me. One photo of a crazy uncle had us laughing so hard, tears were streaming down our face. Photos of a mountain cabin we went to every summer brought back a whole hour of good memories."

I am so grateful he got back in touch to share the life-changing potential of those phrases, "How would I feel?" and "How would I like to feel?" Impatience = disconnection. Those questions can help you fast-forward through frustration and help you listen with empathetic ears.

Why Giving Intrigued Attention Is a Gift

Listening is a magnetic, creative force. The friends who listen to us are the ones we move toward, and we want to sit in their radius. When we are listened to, it creates us, makes us unfold and expand.

PSYCHIATRIST KARL MENNINGER

When my son Andrew was in his early twenties, he started a nonprofit in Washington, D.C. Andrew was able to schedule a fifteen-minute meeting with the director of Howard University, Roberta McLeod, to ask if they could use their campus center for a Holiday for Hope Program.

Three minutes into the meeting, Andrew realized Mrs. McLeod was being polite, but she was waiting for him to stop talking so she could tell him this wasn't going to happen. He imagined she was thinking, *You want the center for free?! Do you know we have a waiting list of groups who would love to have this center for free? Do you know how much it actually costs?*

He realized if he didn't do something differently, he was going to get turned down. He looked around her office. Her walls were covered with pictures of her with students who had gone on to become successful business leaders, politicians, educators, and entrepreneurs. Free information.

He stopped talking about what he wanted and switched the focus to her, "Why do you do this?"

She talked about her challenging early years and how getting an education helped her become the person she wanted to be. She spoke of how satisfying it was helping deserving young people get the support and opportunities they deserved. Andrew gave her his genuine attention. When she was finished, he said simply, "That's our goal, too."

She looked at him and then burst out laughing. "Okay, Andrew, you can have the center."

Please note, Andrew did not listen as a *tactic*. He simply realized he was one of hundreds who wanted something from her. When he stopped pitching and started listening, they connected.

Want to know the rest of that story? Howard University has cohosted four Holiday for Hope programs. Hundreds of people have filled the campus center, eating, dancing, singing, celebrating, and being celebrated. And who's been there each year, smiling at what they created together? Andrew and Roberta McLeod.

That example symbolizes why being intrigued enough to really listen creates *enduring* relationships that are a win for all involved. How about you? Who will you be meeting with in the next few days? A VIP client? Corporate sponsor? Potential employer? A long-time employee? Could you put prejudgments aside and really listen to what she thinks, what she wants? Could you give her your undivided attention so she feels she's the most important thing in your world? Doing so is one of the single best things you can do, in our world of disconnection and alienation, to create a meaningful connection that is rare, welcome, and rewarding for both of you.

What if Someone's Not Listening to Me?

One friend, one person who is truly understanding, who takes the trouble to listen to us as we consider our problems, can change our whole outlook on the world.

PSYCHOLOGIST ELTON MAYO

Are you thinking, *Okay, this makes sense, and I try to listen to others. What if they're not listening to me?* The question is, are you using the techniques covered earlier in this book? Ask yourself:

Am I asking "Did you know?" questions to create curiosity and get eyebrows up? (chapter 1)

Have I turned the person's resistance into receptivity by voicing/ removing his or her objections? (chapter 4)

Am I acknowledging he's busy and asking for LESS time than he anticipates? (chapter 10)

If you've done all that and there's still no connection, maybe the person doesn't find what you're saying *relevant* or *useful*. The next section introduces ways to earn attention because people feel their time with you will be productive and yield real-world results.

Action Questions: Listen Like You Like to Be Listened To

When people don't listen, it's not that they don't learn, they just deny themselves tremendous opportunities and glorious choices.

DIRECTOR STEVEN SPIELBERG

1. Who is someone who really listens to you? What makes her such a good listener? How do you feel about her? Who will you give your undivided attention to today?

2. How are you going to "pull an Andrew" and stop talking, put yourself in the other person's shoes, and see it from his or her point of view to give both of you some glorious choices?

3. Review the situation you've identified on your W5 Form. How are you going to hold yourself accountable for giving this person quality attention by:

    L = Looking, leaning, lifting so you feel and look intrigued

    I = Ignoring distractions by thinking, *You're the most important thing in my world*

    S = Suspending judgment with "Give him or her a chance" so you're not jumping to conclusions

T = Taking notes on what lights up your listener and referring back to it to create a connection

E = Empathizing and preventing impatience by asking yourself "How would I feel?"

N = Not using the word *but*—substitute *and* so you're acknowledging, not arguing

Part VII

INTRIGUE

U = USEFUL

If It Isn't Actionable, It Isn't USEFUL

*A real decision is demonstrated by the fact you've taken a new action.
If you haven't taken action, you haven't truly made a decision.*

AUTHOR TONY ROBBINS

The unspoken question many people have in business situations is,

"Why will paying attention to *you*—pay off for *me*?"

This section provides ways to make your interactions useful so there is an ROI (return on intrigue) for all involved.

It also shows ways to help people decide what actions they plan to take so they reap tangible pay-offs from having given you their time, mind, and dime.

Chapter 17

Establish Real-World Relevance

We're all in a race for relevance.

<small>JOURNALIST ELEANOR CLIFT</small>

It's not enough for people to agree with you *in theory*. They must be able to apply what you're saying *in practice*. If what you're sharing doesn't have real-world relevance for them, why should they pay attention? It's simply not a high-enough priority.

When I worked with Dr. Joan Fallon of Curemark on her TEDx talk, we knew it was crucial to establish that her topic of autism is not just something that affects a few people, it impacts the majority of people in the United States. That's why Joan opened with:

How many of you here know someone who has autism? Please raise your hand.

How many of you here know teachers or therapists who work with children who have autism?

How many of you are familiar with the heartbreak and difficulties families encounter when they have a child who has autism?

So, almost all of you raised your hands, and I imagine those of you watching have had similar situations. Autism is on the rise. Just last month, The Centers for Disease Control put the estimates at 1 in 68 children, and 1 in 42 boys diagnosed with autism. To put that in perspective, that represents an almost 80 percent increase in autism in just ten years. We have an epidemic on our hands. We . . .[30]

Dr. Fallon then went into detail about how Curemark has developed a treatment for autism that is producing such promising results in its clinical trials that it is being fast-tracked by the FDA.

Clarify How This Relates to Your Audience

Do you know the number-one prerequisite for change? A sense of urgency.
AUTHOR JOHN KOTTER

In one brilliantly crafted minute, Joan took her topic out of the abstract and made it pertinent to everyone in the room by:

- Asking people to raise their hands. This request (done genuinely instead of gratuitously) physically involved people and created a visual epiphany where audience members looked around and saw for themselves that almost everyone in the room had their hand up.

- Giving a shout-out to her video audience so they felt involved and "seen." Virtual viewers often feel ignored and distant because they're not "there." Joan connected with virtual viewers so they felt she was talking to them, even if they weren't in the room that day.

- Creating a sense of urgency and gravitas by sharing startling research from a trustworthy source proving this situation is getting worse, not better.

How about you? How are you going to take your topic out of the abstract and make it pertinent to everyone who hears, sees, or reads it? How will you make it so relevant that people are motivated to put other things aside and give you their full "tell me more" attention?

What if People Find What You're Saying Irrelevant?

When are you going to understand that if it doesn't apply to me, I'm not interested.

ACTRESS CANDACE BERGMAN AS MURPHY BROWN

People don't just care whether what you're saying is relevant to *them*, they also care whether what you're saying is relevant to the *situation*. I attended a local political rally where a candidate spent his entire twenty minutes complaining about schools in America and what a shame it was teachers didn't get paid what they were worth. Everyone agreed with his point, but he was a county politician. Even if elected, he would have no budget authority over the education system in the county, much less the country. The crowd got increasingly impatient because he wasn't in a position to correct the problem he was complaining about. His pontificating had no relevance. A man next to me muttered, "What a waste of breath." Agreed.

How can you tell if people are finding what you're saying relevant? Just pay attention to their body language. If you start to see a lot of furrowed eyebrows, shifting in the seats, and digital devices in use, people either don't understand what you're saying or don't find it intriguing or relevant.

If that happens, don't continue with your planned remarks. You've lost their attention and won't get it back by sticking to your script. Interrupt yourself and say, "You may be wondering how this is relevant to _____ (fill in your purpose or theme)." Then clarify how you and they are in a position to take action on this issue, so they're back to trusting this is a productive use of time.

For example, that politician could have saved the day as soon as he saw people's attention wandering. He could have said, "You may be wondering, as a county supervisor, how I would be in a position to impact teacher salaries in our area. Well, I have already met with three members of our board of education and proposed a plan whereby…"

That would have gotten people's attention because it was *prescriptive* (outlining a solution) instead of simply being *descriptive* (outlining a problem). People will only listen so long to how awful something is before they get antsy. They want to know, What are *you* going to do about it? and What can *I* do about it?

Make Your Concepts Concrete

My success in any given class was almost wholly based on how well I could remember the definitions of countless terms—like the precise meaning of 'computer science' or how to explain 'project management' in paragraph form, or the all-too-subtle differences between marketing *and* advertising.

OWNER OF PLATO WEB DESIGN CASEY ARK

In a thought-provoking *Washington Post* article,[31] Casey Ark revealed that, even though he studied computer science (supposedly a smart major given it's one of the ten fastest-growing occupations), what he learned was either obsolete or useless on the job. "My success in any given class was almost wholly based on how well I could remember definitions of countless terms, such as how to explain 'project management' or the subtle differences between marketing and advertising."

Casey said it was a rude awakening to enter the real world of business and discover that employers did not care about his ability to *define* things; they cared about his ability to *do* things.

Part of being intriguing in the business world is understanding we have a responsibility to not talk ad infinitum about concepts that don't contribute to the bottom line. Concepts may be true, but they don't tell or teach people what to do. If we want people's attention, it's our responsibility to make our rhetoric real by stating when and where this happened and what was said.

Want an example of how to make concepts concrete and your rhetoric real?

> **Rhetoric:** *"It's important to protect your company computers from being hacked."*

> **Real world:** *"Last Monday, a department store called in a state of panic. Their head of security told me, 'Some hacker just stole all our customers' credit card information from the past three years.' Our team was on site within the hour, and we were able to identify the source of the leak and take these three steps to fix it and reestablish their security."*

> **Concept:** *Be sure to make customers feel welcome.*

> **Concrete:** *Follow what I call the ten-ten rule when greeting customers. Walk to within ten feet of them with a smile and ask, "How may I serve you?" If you're on the phone or with another customer, look the person in the eye, smile, and say, "I'll be with you as soon as I finish here." Our studies show people will gladly wait up to ten minutes as long as you acknowledge them within the first ten seconds."*

> **Abstract idea:** *It's your job as a manager to hold employees accountable for being on time.*

> **Empirical example:** *"The first time an employee is more than fifteen minutes late, speak to the person in private about it, and this is what you say. . . . The second time, this is what you do. . . ."*

> **Concept:** *We can't really predict the future.*

> **Concrete:** *At SXSW in Austin, Nate Silver gave this example of why, as he said, "There's always the risk of unknown unknowns."*

Do not be content to stop at sharing concepts, theories, rhetoric. Specify *when* and *where* this took place and *what was said or what should be said*. Now you're talking real world. Now people will be able to relate what you're saying to their actual circumstances instead of your words floating in space, serving no practical purpose. Grounding neck-up ideas in *when* and *where* ramps up your relevance because people see where your concept has produced, or can produce, concrete results.

Do You Have the Skills to Pay the Bills?

At the moment of truth, there are either reasons or results.
AVIATION PIONEER CHUCK YEAGER

I enjoy watching the TV show *So You Think You Can Dance* because it features people who are betting on themselves. Despite the odds against "making it" in that notoriously tough industry, these dancers are going all in on their talent and pursuing what they believe they were born to do.

After watching eventual 2014 winner Ricky masterfully deliver an out-of-genre Bossa Nova, judge Mary Murphy burst out with, "You have the skills to pay the bills!" In other words, Ricky will always have paying work because his diverse range of talent makes him highly "hireable" to choreographers who can be confident he'll be able to deliver their vision with excellence.

If you want people to pay attention to you, it's important to emphasize how what you're saying will pay off for them, in the real world. Those are skills that will pay your bills. Yes, INTRIGUE is about earning people's attention; it's also about helping them produce bottom-line results.

The next chapter offers more ways to be prescriptive so you're providing a variety of relevant options people can take to get tangible benefits because they spent their attention on you.

Action Questions: Establish Real-World Relevance

Please take out your W5 Form. Choose to do at least one of the items on this relevancy checklist so people are motivated to put things aside and give you their full attention because they're clear this has practical, real-world value for them. Could you:

1. Ask a series of "How many of you have been in this situation?" questions to give people opportunities to self-identify with your issue or topic?

2. Ask people to raise their hands to physically involve them and create a visual epiphany so they see with their own eyes they're one of many people affected by this issue?

3. Introduce just released research that shows this issue is getting dramatically worse so people feel a sense of urgency and are motivated to pay attention and act *now*?

4. Read your audience's expressions and address impatience by integrating, "You may be wondering how this is relevant to ..." so people are clear about how this is pertinent to them.

5. Make your rhetoric real by referencing when and where this has happened, so they see how your concept has produced concrete results elsewhere and can for them, too?

Chapter 18

Offer Options, Not Orders

Without reflection, we go blindly on our way, creating unintended consequences and failing to achieve anything useful.

AUTHOR MARGARET J. WHEATLEY

It's important to be intriguing, but it's not enough. The question is, to what purpose? Being intriguing is the means; mutually beneficial connections and useful results are the end.

Yet we can't assume people will be motivated to follow up on what we suggest and take action on their own. How many times have you attended a program, left all fired up and raring to go, yet a week later everything was back to same-old, same-old?

That's what will happen unless we follow Meg Wheatley's advice and reflect on how to make our interactions useful so people start, stop, or do something differently as a result of our interaction.

To do this, we need to switch people from a passive, observational mode ("I understand what you mean") to a productive, action mode ("Here's what I'm going to do about this").

See the difference? When people are in the passive, observational mode, the buck *stops* there. When they switch to a productive, action mentality, the buck *starts* there.

Are You Leaving Results to Chance?

Superhuman effort isn't worth a damn if it doesn't produce results.
EXPLORER ERNEST SHACKLETON

The following example shows what happens, or what *doesn't* happen, when someone simply delivers a message and assumes people will take it upon themselves to turn it into results.

The keynote speaker for an international conference spoke about the years he invested in his quest to qualify for the Olympic Games, of choking and not making the finals, of quitting the sport in disgust, then deciding to give it one more try and ultimately winning a medal. End of story.

The audience gave him polite applause, but that was it. It was an okay "speech" but never once did he segue back to the audience and ask how they could apply what they'd just heard to their lives. He never asked:

- "Have you ever worked hard for a goal?"
- "Did you encounter setbacks along the way? What was that like?"
- "Did you throw in the towel or keep going despite the obstacles?"
- "How did it feel to finally achieve what you'd worked for?"

He never made *his* story *our* story. He just talked about himself. He kept his audience in observer mode, focused on what he had done instead of what they could do.

Make Your Insights Applicable
with "You Questions"

Never stop questioning.

SCIENTIST ALBERT EINSTEIN

If only that Olympic athlete had asked a few "you questions." "You questions" are the easiest way to switch from *our* point of view to our *audience's* point of view. They're a way of "turning back" the conversation to our group and transitioning them from thinking, *That was an okay speech* to *How can I apply this or put this into practice in my life?* How do you come up with "you questions"? Ask:

♦ What are the main themes of my message? (For that athlete, it was following your *dream*, overcoming *obstacles*, and the rewards of *perseverance*.)

♦ Have *you* ever worked hard for a *dream*? Poured your heart and soul into something?

♦ Did *you* encounter *obstacles* along the way? Were you tempted to throw in the towel?

♦ Did *you* persevere no matter what? What happened as a result?

♦ What did *you* learn from that experience? What would you do the same? Differently?

Do you see how "you questions" shift the attention from your experience to theirs? People are no longer emotionally distant and passively listening to you talk. They're linking and thinking where this has happened to them in the past or where it's happening to them now. They're remembering how it felt, reflecting on lessons learned, and imagining how they'd change things if they have the chance. That is connection … and it can happen in seconds.

What Action Do You Want Them to Take?

People who develop the ability to continuously acquire
new forms of knowledge they can apply to their work and
lives will be the movers and shakers in our society.

AUTHOR BRIAN TRACY

Remember when we discussed coining a rally cry in chapter 11? Another way to leverage the enduring impact of your phrase-that-pays (e.g., "Click It or Ticket" and "we will prevail") is to make sure it has a verb in it that articulates a constructive action people can take. A pithy sound-bite can be a verbal prompt that reminds people how they want to apply new knowledge.

For example, Sheryl Sandberg's meme "Lean In" has triggered a national conversation because it captures in *two words* a behavior she believes can help your career. When speaking and writing about her topic, she can leverage her phrase-that-pays by adding "you questions" that make the message universally relevant and that transform *her* insight into *her audience's* insight by asking: Are you *leaning in* or leaning out at work? Think of the last staff meeting you attended. Did you contribute to the conversation or lean back and leave without saying anything? How about a committee you're part of. Are you proposing possible solutions or keeping a low profile? Have you ever stopped to think that whether you receive a deserved promotion, project-lead, or pay-raise is directly related to whether you're *leaning in* or leaning out?

Referencing your rally cry throughout your message reinforces it and increases the likelihood people will remember it, share it, and more importantly, act on it.

For example, imagine Neil Gaiman is being interviewed on TV about *Make Good Art*. He could make his message even more actionable by hooking and hinging it to viewers with "you questions." After sharing the Stephen King story of how he arrived at his epiphany, he

If It Isn't Actionable, It Isn't USEFUL

could ask, "Do you ever worry about what could go wrong? Do you get wrapped around the axle about things you can't change? Are you letting the haters get to you? You might want to ask yourself, 'What can I control? I can make good art. That's what I can do.'"

There is a litmus test to determine whether your rally cry is having its intended impact. Just ask people, "What do you remember from what I said or what you read?" or "What were you inspired to do differently?" If the majority can't repeat anything from your work or they can't pinpoint something they changed as a result of your work, it didn't work.

Cause a Shift

"What time is it?" "You mean now?"
BASEBALL PLAYER YOGI BERRA

The theme of this section is that it isn't enough to get someone's attention, the goal is to cause a shift, *now.* Yet many communications end with a whimper. Many people wrap up with a simple, "Thank you for listening" or "I appreciate your time." Talk about leaving results on the table.

If you want people to reap tangible results, you can't afford to be subtle. Ask questions that plant specific action seeds that prompt people to clarify exactly when, where, and how they're going to apply this to improve their life and the lives of others. Sample Action Questions include:

- "What is one thing you'll do differently when you get back to the office tomorrow?"
- "What exactly are you going to say if this person interrupts you again?"
- "When you get home tonight, where are you going to post your reminder card?"
- "At our next break at 2:30, …"

In fact, planting the action seed "At our next break at 2:30 . . ." helped an entrepreneur named Marcia motivate some presentation-weary investors to follow up with her. Marcia was scheduled to speak after lunch. She was worried audience members would be suffering from the afternoon blahs, so we crafted a sixty-second close to make sure people wanted to connect with her afterward. Here's what she said, then I'll show how to adapt this close for your purposes.

- "I'm Marcia, the one with the white, spiky hair.

- At our next break at 2:30, I'll be at our booth in the right-hand corner of the lobby.

- If you'd like a product demonstration, a copy of our financial projections, or would like to meet our CTO to discuss our patented software, you're welcome to visit our booth.

- Once again, I'm Marcia with the white, spiky hair. I look forward to seeing you at 2:30."

Guess who was *surrounded* by people at the next break? You're right, Marcia. Why? She was the *only one* who gave three specific ways and reasons to follow up with her. She:

- Repeated her name in her close to imprint it (Think about it. After a long day, how many speakers' names can you recall?)

- Made a visual self-reference so she stood out in the crowd (This is not trivial. How will people be able to pick you out in a sea of suits unless you give them a colorful clue such as, "I'm Bob, the one in the green jacket" or "I'm Patricia, the one with the unique hat.")

- Identified a specific time and location where people could connect with her (This is too important to leave to chance. Say, "I'll be by the front desk from 3:00 to 4:00 pm." Or "You're welcome to call me during office hours on Monday between 10:00

and noon." Or "I'll be back in Texas September 3rd and would be glad to schedule an in-person appointment.")

♦ Offered three incentives for continuing the conversation (Far too many people trail off with a vague, "Please let me know if you have any questions.")

Suggest Sample Responses

If you don't like what's being said, change the conversation.
DON DRAPER, *MAD MEN*

Want another way to help people get real-world results? Instead of telling them, "You need to change," suggest what they can say *differently* so they know *how* to make that change.

If people don't know what to say, they often don't say anything at all. For example, when I speak at leadership programs for women, I'm often asked "Why are women so catty to one another?"

My response? "In my opinion, every time we ask or answer that question, we perpetuate that negative stereotype. We do not help our cause when we call one another names. If our goal is to support one another, it's time to change this narrative. Here's how we can do that."

If someone says, "Why are women so catty to one another?" or any variation on that theme, do *not* repeat the unwanted word. Every time we do, we imprint the very thing we don't want. It's like telling kids, "Don't run around the pool." What are they going to do? *Run around the pool.*

Instead say, "You know what I've found? I've found women to be amazingly supportive of one another. In fact . . ." and then share an example of how a woman mentored or championed you. The only way to reverse this unhelpful perception is to stop complaining about it and create a new story about how women elevate and celebrate one another. That's what we want, right?

Notice I didn't share a platitude such as "Don't take it personally." Platitudes frustrate people because they're surface advice. It's more helpful to offer sample dialogue of what to say when you find yourself in that situation. Sample responses jump-start people's confidence because they can "use their words" instead of being tongue-tied or tongue-twisted.

Want another sample response for the "catty women" question? Quote *Saturday Night Live* alum Amy Poehler who said this to a reporter who asked, "Are you bothered by bossy women?"

Amy said, "I just love bossy women. To me, bossy is not a pejorative term. It means somebody's passionate and engaged and ambitious and doesn't mind leading."[32] Go Amy.

The transformative impact of providing sample responses was brought home to me when a workshop participant raised her hand and said, "I never liked it when women called one another catty or bossy, but I never spoke up because I didn't know what to say. Now I have options."

That's the power of sample responses. They help people speak instead of turning the other cheek.

Help People Turn Intentions into Actions

Life is what happens to you while you're busy making other plans.
MUSICIAN JOHN LENNON

Wouldn't it be wonderful if we all did what we intended to do? Yet you know what happens. Life. Here's another way to help people turn their good intentions into actions and results. Collect and share your own top ten "take action quotes." Suggest people post them in-sight, in-mind. It may be just the incentive they need to overcome procrastination. Here are my top ten:

1. "Discipline is remembering what you want."

   —POSTER IN GYM

2. "At the moment of truth, there are either reasons or results."

   —PILOT CHUCK YEAGER

3. "I have heard every excuse in the book—except a good one."

   —FITNESS COACH BOB GREENE

4. "I'd rather regret the things I've done than regret the things I didn't do." —ACTRESS LUCILLE BALL

5. "Action is the antidote to despair."

   —SINGER JOAN BAEZ

6. "A year from now, you will wish you had started today."

   —RUTH REED (SAM'S MOM)

7. "Life loves to be taken by the lapel and told, 'I'm with you kid, let's go.'" —MAYA ANGELOU

8. "Life expands or contracts in proportion to one's courage."

   —AUTHOR ANAÏS NIN

9. "If you want more luck, take more chances."

   —AUTHOR BRIAN TRACY

10. "Let us, then, be up and doing, …"

    —POET HENRY WADSWORTH
    LONGFELLOW

Why Is It Advantageous to Give Options, Not Orders?

People are usually more convinced by reasons they discovered themselves than by those found by others.

AUTHOR BLAISE PASCAL

You may be thinking, *These suggestions make sense, but why did you name this chapter, "Offer Options, Not Orders?"* Good question. Please review the techniques in this chapter. Do you notice a pattern? None of the suggestions involve giving orders where you *tell* people what they *should* do or *ought* to do. Do you know anyone who likes to be ordered around? I didn't think so.

Telling people, "You need to …," "You have to …," "You must …," You should …," elicits a "Grrr …" gut feeling or a "You're not the boss of me" internal response. The suggestions in this chapter involve giving a variety of "You might want to …" options so people have the autonomy to select or discover the ones that are most appealing and pertinent to *them*.

The goal of INTRIGUE is not to control or manipulate people to do what *you* want them to do. It is to provide action options that give people the freedom to decide for themselves how they want to proceed or follow up because they want to, not because they're being told to.

Action Questions: Offer Options, Not Orders

I always say don't make plans; make options."

ACTRESS JENNIFER ANISTON

1. Please review your W5 Form. What "you questions" will you ask, what options will you offer, so people have the autonomy and incentive to follow up in ways useful to them?

2. What dialogue phrases and sample responses will you suggest so people know exactly what to say and how to handle a challenging situation more effectively?

3. What inspiring quotes are you going to introduce to help people overcome procrastination and turn their good intentions into real-world results?

Part VIII

INTRIGUE

E = EXAMPLES

Don't Tell Stories; Share Real-Life Examples

In influencing others, example is not the main thing; it's the only thing.
HUMANITARIAN ALBERT SCHWEITZER

In this section, you'll discover that illustrating your ideas with re-enacted examples is one of the single best things you can do to connect with people.

Why can we read novels for hours at a time and it's not hard work?

It's because authors put us in the scene so we're there. They reenact conversations so we care.

This is the opposite of INFObesity, defined by Macmillan Dictionary as "the condition of continually consuming large amounts of information, especially when this has a negative effect on a person's well-being and ability to concentrate."

Learning how to replace INFObesity with reenacted true examples will help your communication come alive so it becomes real.

Replacing INFObesity with reenacted true examples helps your communication come alive so it becomes real, and is the key to influencing with integrity.

Chapter 19

Illustrate Ideas with Dog on a Tanker Examples

When you start to develop your powers of empathy and imagination, the whole world opens up to you.

ACTRESS SUSAN SARANDON

A fascinating article in the *Washington Post* opened my eyes to how helping people imagine a situation helps them empathize with it. An oil tanker had caught fire eight hundred miles off the Hawaiian coast. A cruise ship going by made a daring rescue and was able to save the eleven crew members.[33]

The captain held a press conference and said how grateful he and his crew were to be rescued, but all he could think about was his dog Hokget who'd been left behind, abandoned on the tanker.

That press conference with the captain's poignant story about his dog went viral. Donations started pouring in from around the world. $5. $500. $5000 (!).

The US Navy changed the exercise area of the Pacific Fleet to search fifty-thousand square miles of open ocean in an effort to find the tanker. They actually found the tanker and sent a C-130 to fly low over it to see if there was any sign of Hokget.

Sure enough, there was a brown-and-white blur racing frantically up and down the deck. Miraculously, after being adrift for twenty-five days, Hokget had survived. The US Coast Guard launched a quarter-of-a-*million* dollar (!) mission to rescue Hokget. Against all odds, they were able to safely bring him back to Hawaii.

Are you thinking, *Good for Hokget, but what's that got to do with con-necting with people?*

Here's the question. Why did people from around the world mobilize to save *one dog*, when there are thousands of people in their own cities, states, and countries who need food, water, shelter?

As Shankar Vedantum, author of the article, explains, it's because of something called the *Empathy Telescope*. The Empathy Telescope is a psychological phenomenon that states, "It's easier to care about *one* person than it is *many*."

Why? We can put ourselves in the shoes of one person. We can imagine and empathize with that person's situation. We can see it, relate to it, identify with it. That's *doable*. We cannot put ourselves in the shoes of millions. Our mind (and heart) can't conceive, comprehend, or picture mass numbers. That's *daunting*. One person is relatable—a magnitude of many is not.

What does this mean for you? You can be the world's top authority on a subject, but people may not find it intriguing unless you *illustrate* your idea by embedding in it an example of *one* person who experienced what you're talking about and knows firsthand how valuable your solution is.

Can People Picture What You're Saying?

The soul never thinks without a mental picture.
PHILOSOPHER ARISTOTLE

I sat next to someone new at a National Speakers Association luncheon. I introduced myself, "I'm Sam Horn, the Intrigue Expert." He said, "I'm Tom Tuohy. I run Dreams for Kids."

(Hint. Want to bypass chit-chat? Don't ask, "What do you do?" That elicits INFObesity. Ask, "What's *an example* of what you do?" so people skip the job description and jump into a Dog on a Tanker story.)

With that in mind, I asked Tom, "What's an *example* of what Dreams for Kids does?"

Tom thought about it and said, "Well, here's this young man named JJ. When he was seventeen, he was playing hockey, got blocked into the boards, broke his neck, and became an instant quadriplegic.

"After months of surgeries and rehab, JJ became active in our Extreme Recess programs. But his *real* dream was to go to Mexico for spring break so we made that happen for him. On our last day there, JJ saw a brochure about swimming with dolphins. He told me, 'I want to try that.'

"So we took JJ to the dolphin facility. And with me supporting him on one side and Dick supporting him on the other side, we took JJ into the pool. The trainer let in a female dolphin. She swam slowly around our group, and then stopped right in front of JJ and scanned him with her sonar. She got visibly agitated, probably because her sonar was picking up there was something different about his body and she couldn't figure it out.

"The more upset the dolphin got, the more upset JJ got. He looked up at me and said, 'I don't want to cause problems, just take me out of the pool.'

"Thankfully, the trainer was a compassionate guy. He said, 'Wait. Let's bring in her boyfriend and see what happens.' He let in the male dolphin. He too swam around the group, stopped in front of JJ, and scanned his body. He got kind of hyper, swam over to the female dolphin, and they started click-clicking away.

"JJ, who has quite a sense of humor, smiled and said, 'Guess who they're talking about?'

"Then, a miracle happened. The female dolphin swims over to JJ, stands up on her tail, leans in, and gives him a kiss."

How Telling a Dog on a Tanker Story Elicits Empathy

If we go on explaining, we shall cease to understand one another.

FRENCH DIPLOMAT TALLEYRAND

Are you wondering, *That's a moving story, but what does it have to do with The Empathy Telescope?*

Are you involved with a philanthropic cause or charity? If so, you know some are struggling financially these days. They've been hard hit by the tough economy, and many corporate sponsors have cut back on their donations.

Many nonprofit leaders go to public showcases where they have a five- to ten-minute opportunity to get in front of dozens of foundation executives and philanthropic executives to make their case for why they deserve financial support in the coming year.

Tom goes to as many of these as he can in an ongoing effort to raise money to support Dreams for Kids' expansion of its programs and services. What happens is, everyone else puts up their PowerPoint slides and starts talking about their allocation of funds and the *many* people they've served. When it's Tom's turn, he simply tells JJ's story.

In the last thirty seconds of his time, he lets people know Dreams for Kids has helped five thousand kids just like JJ. And for an investment of $100 per child, they can make it possible for other kids like JJ to get off the sidelines and into the games of life, to go adaptive water-skiing, horseback riding, and at the next break, he'd be glad to talk with them about how to do that.

At the end of a l-o-n-g day of presentations, who do you think those decision-makers relate to? Who do they remember? Who do they walk up to and choose to fund?

Please note, I am *not* saying those other organizations aren't worthy. I'm saying that information can come across as wah-wah rhetoric. Explanations don't cause people to feel. Logic can leave people cold. Audiences care about people not points.

Are You Using Dog on a Tanker Examples when You Communicate?

It is the function of art to renew our perception. The writer shakes up the familiar scene, and, as if by magic, we see a new meaning in it.

AUTHOR ANAÏS NIN

Did you know the title of Vedantum's article? It was *Genocide and Famine*? Would you have read that article? As vital as it was, Vendantum understood some people might have opted out unless he shook things up and helped them perceive that dark topic in a new light. By opening with that Dog on a Tanker example, he helped readers understand that if we want people to care about an issue (whether that's genocide, famine, or people with disabilities) it's better to share an example of one person so people can empathize with our issue instead of be overwhelmed by it.

What does this mean for you? What is your big idea, issue, cause? The more you try to tell people how dire this situation it, how many thousands of people are being affected, the more you will chase people away. Instead, ask yourself, *Who is a walking-talking example of someone who proves my premise? Who is the poster child of what I want to get across?*

How Do I Come Up with My Dog on a Tanker Example?

Good fiction creates empathy. A novel takes you somewhere and asks you to look through the eyes of another person, to live another life.

AUTHOR BARBARA KINGSOLVER

Are you thinking, *Okay this makes sense, but are you really suggesting we don't tell stories?* I like stories as much as the next person, but do you know what I've found in my twenty years of coaching people to make their written and spoken communications more compelling?

Despite a growing acknowledgment of the power of storytelling in business, many professionals still think stories are something Disney does, something you tell around campfires or to your kids at bedtime. Whether it's fair or not (and it's not), some decision-makers still perceive stories as "fluff" and feel they have no place in business communications because they're something you *make up*. At some level they're thinking, *If you made this up, what else are you making up?*

That's why I emphasize illustrating your ideas with true examples that actually happened. How do you find examples? Keep your antennae up for situations that offer social proof of what you want to say. Anyone who has spent time around me can vouch for my frequent use of "sixty-second examples." Offering a quick example of someone who has done what I'm talking about, successfully, is a shortcut to people saying, "I see now."

Please pull out your W5 Form. What is the primary point you want people to understand, care about, connect with, act on? Who is:

- ◆ ONE person who overcame a challenge because he or she acted on your idea?

- ◆ ONE customer who is better off because of your company?

- ONE client who solved a problem because of your product?
- ONE association member who got involved in your organization and is now thriving?

What is the Hero's Journey arc of that person? In case you're not familiar with Joseph Campbell's work on the Hero's Journey, it is a story structure many novelists and screenwriters use in which the lead character leaves home, faces adversity, ultimately triumphs, and returns home victorious.

Your Dog on a Tanker example is essentially a Hero's Journey story of one person who overcame a challenge related to your topic. People will identify with what you're saying because they're putting themselves in the shoes of your character and relating to what they went through. They're no longer detached and distant. They now care about what you care about.

Action Questions: Illustrate Ideas with Dog on a Tanker Examples

Maybe part of our formal education should be training in empathy. Imagine how different the world would be if there were "reading, writing, arithmetic, empathy."

ASTRONOMER NEIL DE GRASSE TYSON

1. Look at your W5 Form. What is the main idea you want to get across? What is a true example of someone who was in that situation and ultimately triumphed over it because he or she worked with your company, used your product, hired your services, or acted on your idea?

2. How will you start your communication with an example (not an explanation!) so people are instantly imagining and empathizing with what you're saying?

3. What do you care about that your intended audience doesn't yet care about? Why are people skeptical of that, apathetic about that? When is a time someone else was skeptical or apathetic about a similar situation but was won over and now that person believes in this? How can you turn that into a Dog on a Tanker example that elicits empathy for your issue or cause?

Chapter 20

Put People in the SCENE

The role of the musician is to understand the content of something and to be able to communicate it so it lives in somebody else.

CELLIST YO-YO MA

Someone who is a master at communicating her message so it lives in someone else is sixteen-year-old Nobel Peace Prize winner Malala Yousafzai. Malala, an advocate of education for girls in Pakistan, was shot in the head and neck by a Taliban gunman who boarded her school bus. She has since recovered and become an inspiring champion for the rights of girls.

In an interview on *The Daily Show,* Jon Stewart asked Malala what she would do if she was attacked again by a Taliban gunman. Malala spoke as if the gunman was standing in front of her: "I would tell him how important education is and I would even want education for your children. I would say, 'That's what I want to tell you, now do what you want.'"

The audience gave her a thunderous ovation. Stewart was momentarily speechless, then said, "I know your father is backstage and he's very proud of you, but would he be mad if I adopted you?"[34] You might want to watch this video clip to see how Malala puts people in the scene so they see what she means.

Why Re-Enacting What Happened Creates a Connection

If now isn't a good time for the truth, I don't see when we'll get to it.

POET NIKKI GIOVANNI

Please notice, Malala didn't "tell a story," she re-enacted what happened to her and projected what she would say and do if that happened again.

A nonnegotiable aspect of INTRIGUE is that it's always a good time to tell the truth. It's the only way people can trust us. Re-enacting real-life events creates credibility and commonality. People are no longer wondering if this is something you pulled off the Internet. They are in that situation with you, seeing what you saw, identifying with what happened.

When we put people in the scene with us, they no longer feel isolated, alone; they feel connected because they are part of a shared experience. Okay, enough *explaining* why putting people in the scene is so effective. Here's an example of how to do it, then I'll share five specific steps you can use to put people in the SCENE in your written and spoken communications.

Several summers ago, I got in the zone while working on a book. The days and weeks flew by. Before I knew it, September had arrived and I hadn't gone swimming once. And I live on a lake.

I promised myself that wouldn't happen again. I vowed to swim several times a week. One afternoon, after a long day of consults, I jumped in my van and went "pool shopping." I drove past a pool tucked under some shade trees, impulsively pulled a U, parked, and went in, armed with my goggles for some lapping and a towel for some napping.

As soon as I saw the fountain in the shallow end, I knew I'd found the "family" pool. I settled on a chaise lounge next to a woman watching her three young kids play. A few minutes later, a man wearing a business suit walked in. The three kids bounded out of the pool and ran to meet him.

"Daddee, Daddee." He hugged them, gave his wife a peck on the cheek, and headed to the locker room to change into his swim trunks. Moments later, he was in the pool surrounded by his adoring brood. They were showing him the strokes they'd learned in their swim lessons, diving off his shoulders in the pool, and playing Marco Polo. It did my heart good to know families still play Marco Polo. It was a scene right out of a Norman Rockwell painting.

All of a sudden, he paused, looked at his wife almost in a state of wonder, and said, "Hon, why don't we make this our default? Why don't we just meet at the pool every night after work?"

I have to admit. I held my breath. I looked at her, thinking, *Please say yes.*

She thought about it, smiled in agreement, and said simply, "Why don't we?"

In five seconds, they abandoned an old default and adopted a new default that could forever favorably impact their family. Instead of get up, go to work, go home; it's now get up, go to work, go to the pool, go home. Who knows, they may always remember that as the summer they met Dad at the pool every night, the summer everything was right with their world.

How to Put People in the SCENE

I don't believe people are looking for the meaning of life as much as they are looking for the experience of being alive.
AUTHOR JOSEPH CAMPBELL

Are you wondering, *What does that pool story have to do with connecting with people?* Imagine I wanted to make a point about how many of us are unwittingly undermining our ability to connect with people because we're operating with old defaults. Imagine I wanted to recommend we adopt new defaults to help us create mutually rewarding connections.

I could continue to explain my idea with wah-wah rhetoric, or I could put you in the SCENE of a situation where someone replaced an old default with a new one and benefitted as a result. Which is more engaging, more persuasive?

Here are five specific ways you can make your examples come alive by putting people in the SCENE of an example where someone made the shift you're suggesting. Put us "there" with:

S = Sensory detail: What did it look like, smell like, sound like, feel like? Describe the time, place, and location in just enough vivid sensory detail so we might as well be standing or sitting right next to you because we're seeing in our mind's eye.

C = Conflict: What was wrong? Who is your "lead character?" What was he or she struggling with? What challenge did he or she overcome? Be sure to share the transformative shift so we know what problem the individual was facing and how it was solved.

E = Experience it: Don't tell your example with your mouth; re-experience it in your mind so it's as if it's happening now. Robert Frost said, "No tears in the writer, no tears in the reader." Feel whatever you want the people you're connecting with to feel.

N = Narrative: Why can we read novels for hours at a time and it's not hard work? It's because narrative makes us feel we're right in the middle of the conversation. Narrative is a non-negotiable. Include back-and-forth dialogue ("He said, "I can't believe this is happening." She said, "I can't believe it didn't happen a long time ago.") so it comes alive.

E = Epiphany: What is the lesson learned, the happy ending, the aha where the light comes on, the band plays and it all comes together and everyone gets the point?

A mantra of the speaking profession used to be, "Make a point, tell a story." It's time to update that. In these days of impatience and Attention Bankruptcy, if you take too long to make a point, people will never make it to the story. It's better to put people in the SCENE of a successful shift because it *will make your point for you.*

Action Questions: Put People in the Scene

If there's magic in story-telling, and I'm convinced
there is, the formula seems to lie solely in the aching
urge to convey something you feel is important.
AUTHOR JOHN STEINBECK

How are you going to make your example come alive by putting people in the SCENE so they identify with you and your issue? How will you re-enact a real-life situation where someone successfully overcame a relevant challenge so it comes alive?

- **S = Sensory Detail:** *How will you describe what that situation looked like so vividly we have a "sense of place" and feel like we're standing/sitting right next to you?*

- **C = Conflict:** *How will you identify the challenge or obstacle your "lead character" faced and overcame so we identify with and "feel their pain?"*

- **E = Experience it:** *How will you mentally put yourself back in that situation and relive it so it comes alive in your mind and ours too?*

- **N = Narrative:** *How will you re-create the actual dialogue that took place (even if it was in your head) so it's as if the conversation is happening now.*

- **E = Epiphany:** *How will you bring it home with a lesson learned, happy ending, or moral of the story so we understand what it all means and have an emotional aha?*

Summary and Action Plan: What's Next?

I associate mastery with optimism.
It is the feeling at the start of a project when I believe
my whole career has been preparation for this moment
and I'm saying, Oh, let's begin. I am ready.

DANCER, CHOREOGRAPHER TWYLA THARP

In our final chapter, we review the shifts I hope this book has inspired you to make.

I hope you are optimistic, ready and prepared to put these ideas into practice.

If so, they can help you earn people's attention and connection, and expand your influence – for good.

Chapter 21

Expand Your Influence—For Good

*I've learned that you shouldn't go through life with a catcher's mitt
on both hands; you need to be able to throw something back.*

AUTHOR MAYA ANGELOU

Brené Brown is definitely throwing something back. Just a few years
ago, she was one of 1,276,700 college professors in the United States.
Now, Brené is positively influencing millions with her books, Oprah
Super Soul Sunday interviews and her *Power of Vulnerability* TED talk,
which is one of their top ten downloaded videos[35] ... deservedly so.

I first met Brené at Goddard Space Center's Leadership Collo-
quium. Gail Williams, the organizer of this series, is generous in asking previous speakers to their special events. When she invited me to
attend Brené's program, I RSVP'd an instant yes.

The auditorium was packed. In the first few minutes, Brené set up her
shift from a self-described geek to a whole-hearted mom, shocked to find
herself forever fretting about her kids. She said, "I never used to be a wor-
rier, but once I became a parent, I would stand in my kids' room at night,
watch them sleep, and *weep*. I knew this was illogical. They were perfectly
healthy, yet I was perfectly miserable. This made no sense."

At this point, Brené could have detailed her research of why feelings of love and happiness are often followed by irrational feelings of
fear. She could have gone into the science and psychology of vulnerability and pointed out that even cynics are susceptible to this. Instead,
she put us in the scene of an anecdote to open our eyes to how univer-
sal this phenomenon is.

"Picture this. A family is driving to their grandparents' house Christmas Eve. They're running behind schedule and the parents are snapping at each other. The kids in the back seat sense the tension and try to ease it by singing *Jingle Bells*. The parents look at each other thinking, *What are we doing*?! and start singing along with the kids. There they are, a happy family singing *Jingle Bells* on the way to their grandparents' house. *Then* what happens?"

Guess what most people said? "They get in a car accident."

"Is that what you thought? Do you know what it means? Deep down, you believe happiness is *too good to be true*. Even in the midst of joy, you're waiting for the other shoe to drop."

You could have heard a pin drop. Everyone in that NASA auditorium, from astrophysicists to aeronautical engineers, was 100 percent intrigued. Why did Brené have us at hello? Why has her message resonated with so many people? Why has her career catapulted so meteorically?

Well, for many reasons. As you just experienced, Brené is an expert at putting us in the scene to show us what she means. Brené's 100 percent authentic. Her goal isn't to impress us; it's to connect with us, however, it is not just her eloquence and universally applicable insights that have led to her success. To my mind, it's because she role models all eight ingredients of INTRIGUE.

Raise the Bar for Yourself and Others

When we see ourselves as grateful, healthy, and with a passionate higher vision for our lives, we raise the bar for everyone.
AUTHOR AND HALL OF FAME SPEAKER MARY LOVERDE

Brené exemplifies that if you create an intriguing communication that earns the attention and respect of your intended audience, you can connect with anyone, anywhere, anytime (even with astrophysicists and scientists on the "soft" topic of vulnerability). Brené personifies what can happen with you replace old defaults (INFObesity) that cause disconnection with the new defaults (INTRIGUE) you've learned in this book that create mutually rewarding connections.

INFObesity	INTRIGUE
Intro that loses them at hello	**I**NTRO that has them at hello
True and old	**N**EW and original
Waste time and lose trust	**T**IME-EFFICIENT so win trust
Forgettable, out-of-sight, out-of-mind	**R**EPEATABLE so top-of-mind
Inform, one-way	**I**NTERACT, two-way
Get attention first	**G**IVE attention first
Useless and irrelevant	**U**SEFUL and relevant
Explanations that cause confusion	**EX**AMPLES that cause us to care

How Can You Use INTRIGUE to Expand Your Influence—For Good?

What if I'm not okay being average?
What if I want to be extraordinary?

ACTOR WILL SMITH

Brené has extraordinary influence. Which is a good thing. Please understand, stepping up to expand your influence comes from service, not arrogance. Wanting to make a difference for as many people as possible is a way of honoring life and making the most of it.

Yet I have discovered some people are initially reluctant to do this. During a presentation for a group of women business owners, my topic was how we can increase our impact by speaking, writing, and coaching on our EEE (expertise, experience, epiphanies).

To my surprise, when asked to share a recent success with the group, several people demurred. One said, "Oh I don't think what I have to say is that interesting." Another said, "I haven't had time to prepare." Another, "There's nothing special about what I did." There was an almost across-the-board devaluing of what they had to offer. And these were successful executives. I asked a woman who had organized a well-attended fund-raiser to share her lessons learned. She shrunk back and said, "Oh, I couldn't. I've only been doing this for four months."

I said, "You didn't just think about this or talk about it. You pulled off a highly successful event that drew the PGA commissioner and several senators. Everyone at that event benefitted from what you did, and everyone in this room will benefit from hearing how you did it."

She said, "But I'm not an expert. It seems kind of arrogant to tell people what to do."

"I'm glad you brought that up. Sharing what you've learned is not egotistical or arrogant; it's an *offering.* You are not claiming, 'I'm perfect, I know all the answers.' You're saying, 'This is what I've gone through, and I'm going to share it in the hopes it might have value for you.'"

Have you ever thought of it that way? Lessons learned in your head help no one. We have all experienced something that might have value for others. It's almost selfish to keep insights to yourself. You do not serve when you *step back.* You serve only when you *step up.*"

She got it. She stood up, stepped up, and, in three minutes, told us how she had put that event together. She served the group because everyone benefitted from her sharing her lessons learned.

Lessons Learned in Your Head Help No One

*In the end, I'm not as interested in what you have to
tell or sell as in how you choose to live and give.*
US Senator Cory Booker

How about you? Have you been asked to share your lessons learned at a business meeting or with your professional peers? Did you say, "Who, ME?!"

If someone at work asked you to share your hard-won wisdom with other employees, would you take yourself out of the game? If a TV reporter or print journalist wanted to interview you about your business, cause, or topic, would you step back and say, "No thanks?" Do unrealistic standards or fears you couldn't do it "perfectly" hold you back and prompt you to pass?

No more. This book has given you the tools to communicate what you care about confidently and compellingly so you can connect with anyone, anytime, anywhere. You now know how to get people's eyebrows up in the first minute. You know how to introduce something new so people want to hear more. You know how to win trust by keeping it brief. You know how to share real-life examples in a way that adds tangible value to others. You know how to live and give back. You have an opportunity, an obligation, to use your new skills to play a bigger game, to expand *your* influence—for good.

What I Wish for You

I wish everyone could get rich and famous and have everything they ever dreamed of so they would know that's not the answer.

ACTOR JIM CARREY

I was raised in a small southern California town (more horses than people) with books as my constant companion. Until age fourteen, I viewed the "big world out there" from an isolated mountain valley. After I graduated from college, fate conspired to land me on Hilton Head Island where I co-managed Rod Laver's tennis resort, which gave me an opportunity to rub elbows with the "rich and famous."

Much to my surprise, as Jim Carrey pointed out, even though many of these movie stars, well-known models, and captains of industry had external success, they were not happy. I discovered firsthand that wealth, fame, awards, acquisitions, and accolades aren't the answer. What is?

Connection. We end as we began. At the end of your life, what will matter? Did you add value and make a positive difference? Did you reach out instead of retreat? Did you give your attention to who and what really mattered? Did you connect with the people important to you?

If You Want to Succeed; Choose to INTRIGUE

You don't have to be a genius or a visionary or even a college graduate to be successful. You just need a framework and a dream.

FOUNDER OF DELL COMPUTERS MICHAEL DELL

This book has given you a framework for *earning* the attention and respect of others. It has given you a recipe for creating mutually rewarding connections. These INTRIGUE ingredients can help you give people your appreciative, undivided attention so they're motivated to respond in kind. They can help you create "all ships rising" experiences where people contribute to and connect with one another so all involved are elevated.

If your dream is to make a positive difference, to leave an enduring legacy of mutually rewarding connections with people on and off the job, you might want to print the "Intrigue Creed" (see page 186) and keep it in-sight, in-mind so these approaches stay top-of-mind.

Reviewing this creed on a daily basis can center you in your commitment to be more intrigued and intriguing. It can help you create relevant communications that people gladly pay attention to because they trust you'll be a productive use of their time. The ingredients in this creed can help you be that rare person who focuses on what others want, need, and deserve first. Your success and satisfaction in life is directly proportionate to the quality of the connections you make. If that's your hope, your dream, choose to INTRIGUE. Everyone, including you, will benefit.

Action Questions: Expand Your Influence—For Good

To change one's life, start immediately, do it flamboyantly, no exceptions.
PSYCHOLOGIST WILLIAMS JAMES

1. Review your W5 Form. How will you bake all eight ingredients of the INTRIGUE recipe for connection into your interaction to increase its likelihood of success?

2. Who is someone you regard as a walking-talking role model of INTRIGUE? Describe that person and why you respect his or her ability to earn attention and connect with anyone.

3. Are you ready to step up and contribute at a higher level? How will you expand your influence—for good—by sharing your lessons learned if asked?

4. Where are you going to post the "Intrigue Creed" so you can see it frequently? What else are you going to do (e.g., keep this book nearby so you can continue to reference it?) to replace old defaults with new defaults that help you turn INFObesity into INTRIGUE?

The INTRIGUE Creed

If you want to succeed, choose to INTRIGUE.
SAM HORN

I = **INTRO:** Craft an INTRO that has people at hello. Get eyebrows up. Ask "Did you know?" Show them the fish. Turn a no into a yes. Share what's rare. Psych yourself up, not out.

N = **NEW:** It's not enough to be true; it must be NEW. Keep current. Create the next new thing. Cause aha's with ha ha's. Ink it when you think it. Look at the world with reawakened eyes.

T = **TIME-EFFICIENT:** Win trust by being TIME-EFFICIENT. Keep it brief, or they'll give you grief. Swaddle your communication. Put a ThunderShirt on emails and meetings.

R = **REPEATABLE:** If they can't REPEAT it, they didn't get it. Craft a phrase-that-pays that resonates. Pause and punch. Coin a rally cry with rhythm, alliteration, inflection, and rhyme.

I = **INTERACT:** Don't just inform, INTERACT. Never again deliver an elevator speech. Create mutually rewarding conversations. Set up a scenius so people can contribute and cocreate.

G = **GIVE:** GIVE attention first. Customize to connect. Listen like you like to be listened to. Get out of your head and into the field. Use their language, meet their needs.

U = **USEFUL:** If it isn't actionable, it isn't USEFUL. Establish real-world relevance. Offer options, not orders. Suggest what to say. Plant action seeds. Make concepts concrete.

E = **EXAMPLES:** Don't tell stories, share real-life EXAMPLES. Illustrate Ideas with Dog on a Tanker examples. Put people in the SCENE. Cause people to care with the Empathy Telescope.

The INTRIGUE Quiz

This quick quiz can kick-start your thinking about how well you're able to earn quality attention and create mutually rewarding connections with others.

The questions are associated with the eight ingredients of the INTRIGUE recipe for connection.

If you want to improve your ability in a specific area, just turn to its matching part in the book. For example, if you want to get better at keeping communications concise (question 3); turn to part III of the book to receive pragmatic tips on how to "Win Trust by Being Time-Efficient."

Your business success and personal satisfaction are directly proportionate to your ability to earn favorable attention in today's world of impatience and alienation. This self-assessment is your first step to clarifying next steps on how you can improve relationships on and off the job.

Take the quiz on the next page.

Answer the following questions, rating each answer from Almost Never (1) to Almost Always (5).

Your first answer is usually the correct one because it comes from your gut, not from your intellect.

	Almost Never (1)	Barely Ever (2)	Sometimes (3)	Very Often (4)	Almost Always (5)
1. Can you get people's favorable attention in the first sixty seconds of your communications?					
2. Are you able to pleasantly surprise people by introducing something new, current, or first of its kind?					
3. Do you honor time promises and keep your spoken/written communications concise and to the point?					
4. Do you craft memorable sound-bites people can repeat, word for word, from your message?					
5. When people ask, "What do you do?" does your response create a meaningful conversation?					
6. Are you able to put things aside, listen fully, and give people your undivided attention?					
7. Do your communications motivate people to take action and produce tangible bottom-line results?					
8. Do you replace explanations with real-life examples so your ideas elicit empathy and come alive?					
9. Are you able to win favorable attention and influence people with your communication skills?					
Total Scores:					
Grand Total:					

0–17: Want good news? You're in the right place. Your current communication skills may not be supporting you at the level you want, need, and deserve. You might want to make this book a priority because it can help you create more rewarding relationships on and off the job.

18–34: You are usually able to earn people's favorable attention, and there's room for improvement. You might want to jump to certain chapters that focus on areas of improvement so you can immediately access techniques that can help you connect better in those situations.

35–50: You're an INTRIGUE all-star! Use this book to strategize specific high-stakes communications so you can increase the likelihood of producing desired results for all involved.

Notes

Intro

1. Ryssdal, Kai. "Goldfish have longer attention spans than Americans, and the publishing industry knows it." *Marketplace Business.* 11 February 2014. Web. www.marketplace.org/topics/business/goldfish-have-longer-attention-spans-americans-and-publishing-industry-knows-it.

2. Olds, Jacqueline, and Richard Schwartz. "The Lonely American." *Utne Reader.* April 2009. Web. www.utne.com/mind-and-body/reconnect-tchnology-society-lonely-american.aspx.

Chapter 1

3. Perman, Stacy. "Making a Profit and a Difference." *Business Week.* April 3, 2009. Web. www.businessweek.com/stories/2009-04-03/making-a-profit-and-a-differencebusinessweek-business-news-stock-market-and-financial-advice.

4. Keener, Sean. Web. http://indie.bootsnall.com/.

5. Smith, Jacqueline. "7 Things You Probably Didn't Know About Your Job Search." 16 April 2013. Web. www.forbes.com/sites/jacquelynsmith/2013/04/17/7-things-you-probably-didnt-know-about-your-job-search/.

6. Begley, Sharon. "The Science of Making Decisions." *Newsweek.* 15 March 2011. Web. www.newsweek.com/science-making-decisions-68627.

Chapter 4

7. Wong, May. "Stanford Study Finds Walking Improves Creativity." *Stanford Daily.* 24 April 2014. Web. http://news.stanford.edu/news/2014/april/walking-vs-sitting-042414.html.

Chapter 6

8. Newcomb, Peter, and Keenan Mayo. "How the Web Was Won." *Vanity Fair.* July 2008. Web. www.vanityfair.com/culture/features/2008/07/internet200807.

9. Sorkin, Andrew Ross. "Why Uber Might Well Be Worth $18 Billion." *New York Times DealBook.* 9 June 2014. Web. http://dealbook.nytimes.com/2014/06/09/how-uber-pulls-in-billions-all-via-iphone/.

Chapter 7

10. Horovitz, Bruce. "Quicken Loans' March Game Plan Pays Off." *USA Today.* 1 August 1999: Print.

Chapter 8

11. Weingarten, Gene. "Pearls before Breakfast." 20 July 2007. Web. www.washingtonpost.com/wp-dyn/content/article/2007/04/04/AR2007040401721.html.

12. Whitacre, Eric. "A Virtual Choir 2,000 Voices Strong." 9 March 2011. Web. www.ted.com/talks/eric_whitacre_a_virtual_choir_2_000_voices_strong.

Chapter 9

13. Carlson, Peter. "Sticking to His Guns." *Washington Post.* 22 December 2007. Web. www.washingtonpost.com/wp-dyn/content/article/2007/12/21/AR2007122102520.html.

Chapter 11

14. Giovanni, Nikki. "Transcript of Nikki Giovanni's Convocation Address. 17 April 2007. Web. www.remembrance.vt.edu/2007/archive/giovanni_transcript.html.

15. Shankman, Samantha. "A Brief Bistory of 'What Happens in Vegas Stays in Vegas'." *The Week.* 1 October 2013. Web. http://theweek.com/article/index/250385/a-brief-history-of-what-happens-in-vegas-stays-in-vegas.

16. Lane, Kathy. "National Click It or Ticket Crackdown Kicks Off with Overwhelming Public Support." National Safety Council. Press Release. 17 May 2004. Web. www.nsc.org/Pages/ClickItorTicketCrackdownKicksOffWithOverwhelmingPublicSupport.aspx.

17. Gaiman, Neil. "Make Good Art." University of the Arts. 17 May 2012. Keynote Address. Web. www.uarts.edu/neil-gaiman-keynote-address-2012.

18. Conan, Neal. "Neil Gaiman Turns His Grad Speech Into 'Good Art'." NPR. 14 May 2013. Web. www.npr.org/2013/05/14/183950906/author-neil-gaiman-on-making-good-art.

Chapter 13

19. Fox, Justin. "The Economics of Well-Being." *Harvard Business Review.* January 2012. Web. http://hbr.org/2012/01/the-economics-of-well-being/ar/1.

20. Carducci, Bernardo. "Small Talk Skills Improve with Practice." *Science Daily.* 18 December 2013. Web. www.sciencedaily.com/releases/2013/12/131218170737.htm.

Chapter 14

21. Addley, Esther. "Ellen's Oscars Selfie Most Retweeted Ever—And More of Us Are Taking Them." *The Guardian.* 7 March 2014. Web. www.theguardian.com/media/2014/mar/07/oscars-selfie-most-retweeted-ever.

22. "UPDATE: Oscars Viewership Best Since 2000; 'Kimmel' Post-Oscars Special Snags Best Ever Results." Yahoo. 3 March 2004. Web. https://tv.yahoo.com/photos/oscars-viewership-hits-10-high-kimmel-post-oscars-photo-184533342.html.

23. "Are Companies that Value Employees More Successful?" CBS News. 31 August 2014. www.cbsnews.com/news/are-companies-that-value-employees-more-successful/.

24. Gavett, Gretchen. "What People Are Really Doing when They Are on a Business Call." *Harvard Business Review*. 19 August 2014. Web. http://blogs.hbr.org/2014/08/what-people-are-really-doing-when-theyre-on-a-conference-call/.

25. Ingram, Paul. "Do People Mix at Mixers? Structure, Homiphily, and 'The Life of the Party.'" June 2007. Web. www.columbia.edu/~pi17/mixer.pdf.

26. Krasny, Jill. "It's Official: Networking Makes People Feel Sleazy." *Inc. Magazine*. Print. 4 September 2014. Web. www.inc.com/jill-krasny/why-networking-feels-sleazy.html?cid=sf01002.

Chapter 15

27. Logan, John. "Sting Breaks through His Writer's Block with a New Musical." *Vanity Fair*. June 2014. Web. www.vanityfair.com/culture/2014/06/sting-photo-annie-leibovitz.

Chapter 16

28. "How to Be a Better Listener." The University of Texas at Austin. 10 October 2010. Web. www.utexas.edu/ce/stories/detail/how-to-be-a-better-listener.

29. Simon, Scott. "Adman Was King of One-Liners, but Knew Where to Draw the Line." NPR. 31 May 2014. Web. www.npr.org/2014/05/31/317437696/david-abbott-the-one-liner-king-of-advertising.

Chapter 17

30. Fallon, Joan. "The Power of Disruption." TEDx. May 20, 2014. Web. www.youtube.com/watch?v=l1CvF7w-Dfk.

31. Ark, Casey. "I Studied Business and Programming, Not English. I Still Can't Find a Job." *Washington Post*. 27 August 2014. Web. http://www.washingtonpost.com/posteverything/wp/2014/08/27/i-studied-engineering-not-english-i-still-cant-find-a-job/

Chapter 18

32. Couric, Katie. "Amy Poehler Tells Katie Couric, 'I Just Love Bossy Women!'" *Glamour.* April 2011. Web. www.glamour.com/sex-love-life/2011/04/amy-poehler-tells-katie-couric-i-just-love-bossy-women.

Chapter 19

33. Vendantam, Shankar. "Beyond Comprehension: We Know that Genocide and Famine Are Greater Tragedies than a Lost Dog. At Least, We Think We Do." *Washington Post.* 17 January 2010. Web. www.washingtonpost.com/wp-dyn/content/article/2010/01/11/AR2010011102007.html.

Chapter 20

34. Yousafzai, Malala. Interview. *The Daily Show with Jon Stewart.* Comedy Central. 8 October 2013. Web. http://thedailyshow.cc.com/videos/a335nz/malala-yousafzai.

Chapter 21

35. Brown, Brené. "The power of vulnerability." TEDxHouston. June 2010. Web. www.ted.com/talks/Brené_brown_on_vulnerability.

Acknowledgments

I may not have the best job in the world, but I'm in the running.

NEW YORKER CARTOON EDITOR BOB MANKOFF

Me too. I also feel I have the world's best job because of the quality of people I am privileged to be around every single day. Many of them pitched in to help make this book something I hope makes a positive difference for everyone who reads it.

Much love to my sister Cheri Grimm, for helping run my business for fifteen years and for being a constant source of wisdom and encouragement from the very beginning.

Huge thanks to Scott Ritter, Andrew Horn, and Mo Sahoo for making Intrigue Agency thrive and for providing the quality of service to our clients that keeps them happy... and coming back.

Mahalo to long-time friends Judy Gray, Mary Loverde, and Denise Brosseau, who invested their time and mind into supporting this project and making it better.

Gratitude to my agent Laurie Liss, who is an everflowing fount of wisdom and support.

Appreciation to the Berrett-Koehler team for publishing this book and creating a "scenius" community that supports its authors. The support of Steve Piersanti, Jeevan Sivasubramanian, Michael Crowley, Rick Wilson, Dianne Platner, David Marshall, Katie Sheehan, Kristen Frantz, Marina Cook, Charlotte Ashlock, and many other BK staff members made this book even better.

A loving shout-out to my sons, Tom and Andrew, and the wonderful women in their lives, Patty Casas Horn and Miki Agrawal. It puts the light on in my eyes and a smile in my heart to see you leading happy, healthy, productive lives and contributing at your highest levels with the lights on in *your* eyes.

And thanks to my clients and audience members for allowing me to share your stories so that others can benefit from your successes and lessons learned.

Index

About the Author

 Sam Horn, the Intrigue Expert, is a positioning/messaging/branding strategist with a twenty-year track record of results with such clients as Intel, NASA, Boeing, Cisco, KPMG, British Airways, ASAE, and Entrepreneurs Organization. She was a top-rated speaker at INC 500/5000.

Sam has helped thousands of entrepreneurs and executives (e.g., Jill Nelson, founder of Ruby Receptionists; *FORTUNE Magazine's* 2012 #1 "Best Small Company to Work for in the US"; Charlie Pellerin, project manager of the Hubble Telescope; and Nina Nashif, founder of Healthbox and World Economic Forum Young Global Leader) to create intriguing books, keynotes, and TEDx talks that have helped them scale their influence and impact.

Sam is the author of *POP!, Tongue Fu!®, What's Holding You Back?, ConZentrate,* and *Take the Bully by the Horns,* which have been endorsed by high-profile individuals including Stephen R. Covey, Billie Jean King, John Gray, Tony Robbins, and Ken Blanchard.

Sam is an in-demand media resource whose work has been featured in *Fast Company, The New York Times,* and *The Washington Post.* She's been on every major TV and radio network, including CBS, NBC, ABC, and MSNBC, National Public Radio, *Jay Leno's Tonight Show,* and *To Tell The Truth,* where she and her Tongue Fu!® team stumped the panel.

Sam is the former executive director and 17-year emcee for the Maui Writers Conference, where she worked with top agents/editors and dozens of bestselling authors including Mitch Albom, Frank McCourt, Nicholas Sparks, James Rollins, and Dave Barry.

Sam lives on a lake near Washington, D.C., where she has the best of all worlds. She can hop on a plane to keynote a convention, visit her sons in Houston and NYC, be downtown in a half hour to host a scenius at the National Press Club, or go for a hike on the lake trails near her home. She feels fortunate to do work she loves that matters.

Visit Sam's website at www.samhorn.com.

We Want to Hear from You!

Do you have success stories from applying these INTRIGUE techniques? We'd love to hear how you're earning quality attention and creating meaningful connections. With your permission, we'll feature your examples in our newsletters, blogs, and podcasts. Who knows, you may make our annual INTRIGUE Hall of Fame, and your story will be seen by people worldwide.

Want to arrange for Sam Horn to teach these *Got Your Attention?* techniques to your conference or company? Discover for yourself why audiences rave about Sam's interactive programs that have everyone connecting, contributing, and instantly applying these insights to their priorities.

Would you like to consult one on one with Sam? Contact us so we can find out more about your project goals and explore how our Intrigue Agency team could help you craft intriguing, one-of-a-kind communications and projects that are a strategic ROI for all involved.

Want to interview Sam for your TV show, newspaper, magazine, book club, podcast, or radio show? You can trust Sam to deliver intriguing insights and innovative suggestions that POP!

Curious to see what got our attention this week? Receive curated INTRIGUE best practices by visiting www.samhorn.com and by connecting with us via social media at @SamHornIntrigue (Twitter handle) and www.facebook.com/SamHornIntrigue.

We look forward to hearing from you at info@intrigueagency.com or by phone at 1-800-SAM-3455. Until then, only connect.

Berrett–Koehler
Publishers

Berrett-Koehler is an independent publisher dedicated to an ambitious mission: *connecting people and ideas to create a world that works for all.*

We believe that to truly create a better world, action is needed at all levels—individual, organizational, and societal. At the individual level, our publications help people align their lives with their values and with their aspirations for a better world. At the organizational level, our publications promote progressive leadership and management practices, socially responsible approaches to business, and humane and effective organizations. At the societal level, our publications advance social and economic justice, shared prosperity, sustainability, and new solutions to national and global issues.

A major theme of our publications is "Opening Up New Space." Berrett-Koehler titles challenge conventional thinking, introduce new ideas, and foster positive change. Their common quest is changing the underlying beliefs, mindsets, institutions, and structures that keep generating the same cycles of problems, no matter who our leaders are or what improvement programs we adopt.

We strive to practice what we preach—to operate our publishing company in line with the ideas in our books. At the core of our approach is stewardship, which we define as a deep sense of responsibility to administer the company for the benefit of all of our "stakeholder" groups: authors, customers, employees, investors, service providers, and the communities and environment around us.

We are grateful to the thousands of readers, authors, and other friends of the company who consider themselves to be part of the "BK Community." We hope that you, too, will join us in our mission.

A BK Business Book

This book is part of our BK Business series. BK Business titles pioneer new and progressive leadership and management practices in all types of public, private, and nonprofit organizations. They promote socially responsible approaches to business, innovative organizational change methods, and more humane and effective organizations.

Berrett–Koehler
Publishers

Connecting people and ideas
to create a world that works for all

Dear Reader,

Thank you for picking up this book and joining our worldwide community of Berrett-Koehler readers. We share ideas that bring positive change into people's lives, organizations, and society.

To welcome you, we'd like to offer you a free e-book. You can pick from among twelve of our bestselling books by entering the promotional code BKP92E here: http://www.bkconnection.com/welcome.

When you claim your free e-book, we'll also send you a copy of our e-news-letter, the *BK Communiqué*. Although you're free to unsubscribe, there are many benefits to sticking around. In every issue of our newsletter you'll find

- A free e-book
- Tips from famous authors
- Discounts on spotlight titles
- Hilarious insider publishing news
- A chance to win a prize for answering a riddle

Best of all, our readers tell us, "Your newsletter is the only one I actually read." So claim your gift today, and please stay in touch!

Sincerely,

Charlotte Ashlock
Steward of the BK Website

Questions? Comments? Contact me at bkcommunity@bkpub.com.